Brave Transitions

A Woman's guide for maintaining composure through changes in work and life

KATIE K. SNAPP

with contributions by

Anne Potter Russ and Carol M. Wight

DEDICATION

To women and girls everywhere, whether they be girlie girls,
naïve freshmen, tough broads, scaredy cats, cranky ol' biddies,
caring mothers, trucker mamas, or my best friend gal pals.
This includes my daughters, as well as all the daughters
of Anne and Carol.

To women in tough workplace situations or challenging
personal ones. You get out there and make it happen day after
day. I am in awe of your perseverance and inner strength. I
want you to recognize it more.

We all seem to occasionally suffer from bouts of low self-
confidence. We all seem to "get" one another.

Here's a toast to us all.

CONTENTS

At nearly any point in time, we are each on the verge of a change, like a boulder about to tumble over the edge, but we cling to the cliff. We grab any scrap of the way it was, and we resist. In the least, we delay.

Katie K. Snapp

KATIE K. SNAPP

ACKNOWLEDGMENTS

Thanks Bobby. I know I don't do change perfectly well myself, yet here I am writing about it. Your patience has inspired me.

Thank you Anne and Carol, who always had a positive note to add for the progress of the book.
You are two of my dearest friends.

Thank you, Dr. Krueger, for so many insights and ideas.

And thank you to all my followers, whom we call the Tribe. You Skirt Strategists are the coolest and most with-it girl gang that I know.

HOW TO BEST USE THIS BOOK

Imagine a little boutique in your neighborhood area, owned locally, and offering a stylish and hip range of outfit options. Age appropriate for you, and regularly evolving. You knew when you first walked in that its comfortable size and organized shelves would work for you.

Every little town should have one, away from the big box offerings that become too commonplace. It's the way personalized shopping should be.

Once you have found this little gem, you know it's there as your go-to destination for a unique ensemble or a quick girlfriend gift. You may not investigate each rack when you visit, but instead you gravitate toward what calls to you. The colorful scarves and studded belts may quickly woo you (for me, it's because I don't have to take off other clothes to try them on). The shelf lined with skinny jeans repels you. No shocker there.

Using this book may prove to be the same for you.

Like my first book, *Skirt Strategies: 249 Success Tips for Women in Leadership*, I wanted to offer a format that was easy to jump in and out of. I have never been accused of being linear, something that constantly drove my technical clients crazy.

My argument was that people rarely operate in a linear mode. We may have an intention of going from Point A to Point B, but reality gets in the way. And that's okay …. let it go …something we talk about later in this book.

My books are proving to be the same, and it seems to work for women, who are excellent at multi-tasking. By the way, if you say that you don't consider yourself adept multi-tasking, then you're probably just over-using your natural ability to manage multiple tasks and allowing it to distract you. If you don't manage it, it will manage you.

Talking now about change and how we manage ourselves through it. There isn't a common path that we all follow, so chances are a book wouldn't fit everyone. I like the approach of offering exercises, powerful questions, and other thought-provoking interventions in this book so that you can use what fits you, and skip over other parts.

Think of it as that cute little boutique around the corner that has the scarves and skirts that you love, but never a pair of jeans that fit. I hope this book offers the best in fashion for you.

And speaking of fashionable, you'll see my lifelong friend, Anne Potter Russ, offer up an appropriate lesson through a personal story. Let's just say that I prodded her and her talent for well-expressed anecdotes. Carol's role was to develop the exercises and ask powerful questions, a skill of hers.

GENESIS: SOME WOMEN'S HISTORY

And so it began, from the beginning of time, that women have been different. So different, that it often feels like we women live in a different world than men. Our behavioral patterns are definitely unique to our species. Our fears are distinctive, especially when faced with a transition. In change, we have an ear for what's occurring, sometimes with a more sensitive outlook than is good for us.

Our differences are reflected in many ways.

When we shop, it's like a hummingbird, impatient to find the next honeysuckle bud. We scan, touch, scout, examine, taking into account the options, colors, textures. It's as if we are decorating our world.

Men? They hunt, kill, and drag it home. End of story.

When we transition, we may dart all over the place, feeling unanchored and disoriented.

Now I know these are generalizations. Actually they are

something I call "genderalizations" which is generalizing based on gender. And I know it seems a little dangerous to demonstrate based on the sexes. But when you examine the data, men have general patterns for their behaviors. Women? Same thing. We have evolved over time.

I sometimes get pushback from women when they hear how Skirt Strategies training differentiates between the way a man does something and how we women do something. Their argument is that we are not all that different.

I used to think that, too. It's not that I believed we were the same, it's that I simply did not pay that much attention to it.

Then I began looking at situations more closely. I would ask myself, "Would a man even say those same words?" In fact, if you are one of the believers that women are not that much different than men, keep that question in your hip pocket. In the next situation where you are discussing something that occurred where a man was involved or where you are actually having a discussion with a man, ask it. I dare ya. Just do it.

There are loads of similarities because we are all the same species. Yet, we are all exceptional in our own ways, and it is safe to say that most men are different than most women.

You probably want an example.

Okay, fine. In our dialogue: we can get into the nooks and crannies of a personal dilemma by uncovering the way in which someone said something, and the tone, and the relational history, and SO ON! That "so on" translates to on and on and on. Although I never do that … no.

Let's just start with an actual case. We have all been in the situation where a family member or close friend passed away. Let's say you were at a gathering with colleagues or friends and the mention of Belinda passing away comes up.

Did you analyze how you each reacted to the event? How her passing was more of a life lesson for those of us left behind and you shared your own emotional reactions with each other.

"Oh I know! I can't believe she's gone!"

"I loved the way she looked at life. She was always so positive."

"It's a reminder to me that we should all be that positive. Grieving is nothing more than our own selfish way of responding to the loss. It's us losing."

"I was just at the museum fundraiser with her last week and she looked so healthy."

"Oh I didn't think so. I thought she was pallid. She did not look good to me,"

"Well she never really ate right."

You might expect a "bless her heart" about now.

"Someone told me she was diagnosed with a blood disorder recently? Did you hear that?"

And now let's drift into the "on and on" portion of our story.

"You're kidding? Did she keep it quiet?"

"I don't know. Don't let that get around. It was only a rumor."

"Oh yeah, we don't want to get into rumors."

Then there's the man's version

"That's sad. That's a loss."
"Uh huh"

Now, I happen to be a woman and I love the girl type of dialogue. I think it's interesting, and interactive, and fun, except maybe when it's about death or it's about you behind your back. It's what I look forward to with my girlie friends, both inside and out of work.

And it is no shocker to most of you that many men just don't get it. An inflexible man will be driven crazy by it.

In a workplace environment, I once heard a man say "Okay you hens, break it up and get back to work." This was after walking by a clutch of us in an animated exchange.

Know this. Women communicate in a different way, and it's actually pretty effective. A smart man can use this to his advantage. Men should not try to squash it or change it.

My personal favorite in illustrating the differences is when a conflict occurs among our friends. We examine it as if we were armchair psychologists. We delve into someone's past as a motivation for her present behavior, contending that her sour mood must have deeper roots.

"Well, you know she had a really bitter divorce a couple of years ago,"

Then we either warmly accept her for it or bitterly judge her for it. It's tough out there.

Next, toss in a bottle of merlot and the conversation is fueled for even more scholarly insight.

"She was probably in that sour mood all the time 'cause she doesn't get enough sex."

Yeah, we probably beat the issues to death. But we thrive on the in's and out's of the dynamic of a relationship and the way it evolves.

And so this book will leverage some basic female traits that you exhibit, and in particular, those that you will see during change. Will they all resonate with you in particular? Probably not. But that's okay. This is intended to be therapeutic reading – something that takes you a bit inside yourself for answers.

So for all you women who have reached for this book because you are in some transition, and the word "BRAVE" somehow spoke to you, I want to start with a resounding "GO!

You CAN do this!"

This is my promise to you: once you understand two things, you will find the process of change a cakewalk compared to your past experiences. The two items are:

Change-Management Principle #1
You are stronger than you think. Know it and trust yourself.

Change-Management Principle #2
Change is a process that has some predictable elements. Learning from the past will help you see the disturbance as rather foreseeable, which will lead to a sense of confidence rather than disruption.

Let's get on with it, Braveheart.

Presto! Changing Others

I never really considered the option that a happy marriage could lead to "irreconcilable dishwasher differences." Don't get me wrong, my husband is a great guy, and a really great help around the house. He likes laundry. I know... that should be enough.

But, the way he loads a dishwasher makes me wonder if he really has opposable thumbs. It looks like a possum got in there and scattered bits of dishes about. And, to make it worse, he's an engineer. He ought to understand the efficiency of physics and the loading laws of dishwasher best practices.

Why do I care? I can't get him to change.

There, I said it. HE needs to change. I can do all other marital experiments his way... the garage is his mess, my kitchen table is his office, and electronic cords are his crack cocaine. But the dishes, the dishes... oy vey.

So, I practice in managing my expectations, practice in patience, practice in finding another extension cord to make him happy. But, it's a work in progress, I tell you.

-- Anne

1 THE START OF A JOURNEY

Or maybe a Journal ....

Within each of us is an innate strength that won't show itself until tested. And even then for many of us the first reaction in a pinch is to clench our teeth in a sort of fear. It's not that we don't have the backbone for the challenge, it's that our first response as humans is just that: to clench.

It plays out the same in most life scenarios. We are after all, human.

To set the scene, envision the following:

You're sitting on a park bench on a calm, sunny day, with a few hours to actually spoil on yourself. Your cute little lapdog is at your feet, or fill-in the blank with pet of choice, including parrot on your shoulder or book in lap if you're not a fan of the furry. In the grassy area ahead of you is a small circle of young adults throwing Frisbees back and forth to each other. Their leaping and giggling reminds you of a more nostalgic time in your life as a co-ed on a tree-lined campus. You smile inwardly.

As you relax more, their chatter glides into a rhythmic drone, lulling yourself into a relaxed state where your mind lets go, and your arms fall limp at your sides. It's that pre-nap state where you are somewhat awake, yet dozing a little. You become aware of a chirping in a distant tree, and a buzz of a bee as it passes you. Ahhh.

All at once, a few voices rise, yelling in your direction. "Lookout!"

As if in slow motion, your eyes come to focus, locking on the spinning disk as it whirls your direction. You lift your head slightly, realizing you're in the line of fire. It is slicing through the air on direct track for your forehead and you impulsively let out a defensive yelp. I know these yelps well, for I play competitive sports. I'm a yelper.

For the imaginary scenario, I'll gift you with quick reflexes. We'll say that our story ends without a bruised lump on your forehead. Either way, what would you say was your reaction?

Did you have a heightened heartbeat after ducking? Had your state of relaxation instantly evaporated? And was the bark that came out of your mouth slightly unintended?

All reactionary. All instinctive. None uncommon.

When a certain part of our world shifts, whether work or

personal, we respond in a parallel way yet on a different level. There are reactions that are emitted quickly and without thought, while others may paralyze us.

Women have a way of finding an anchor in the midst of a storm. For all those times where you thought you might buckle and fall into the earth, consider what really happened.

Looking for the right thing

The difference between a pessimist and an optimist is her perspective. The glass is half full, half empty, or it needs more red wine. In change, we can somehow cross over to the negative side. The hidden pessimist in us surfaces its nasty little noggin. Within that, a voice that screams when the road takes a turn.

Our brains work like a programmed computer – we get what we expect. We preemptively see the writing on the wall and so we look for it. We suspect someone will behave a certain way and so we expect her to act that way. We think the Bolognese entrée is a bad idea since we have on our favorite white blouse, and so we focus too much on being careful not to dribble, and so we … well, you know the ending.

Listening Posts and Survival Mechanisms

I had a survival tactic to get my self and my sanity through the middle and upper school years of my children. It was a moms' group that met once every six weeks or so, under the guise of informing each other of wayward science assignments and draconian teachers gone wild. What it really ended up being was a "Me, Too!" fest. You know the drill... "I don't understand the math assignments anymore, they are way beyond me." And the table at the Italian restaurant echoes, "Me, too!!"

We started our group with a name. "Ten And Two." The name was not only our moniker, but the rationale for our existence, as well. When you are driving your kids around in the car, and they actually start talking, just keep your hands on the wheel at 10 & 2, just like driver's ed taught. Keep your mouth shut, and your eyes on the road. You will find out everything you ever needed to know, mostly from your kids' friends, and keep on truckin'.

Keeping our sanity meant keeping our hands on the wheel, our eyes on the prize (graduation) and our ears to the ground at our favorite Italian eatery.

"She said WHAT at the sleepover?" "What sleepover?"

"Who got the part in the play?" "What play, when?"

When I would bring all of my valuable information home to my mildly curious husband, he would just take a deep breath and sit down until I had finished my tirade of "her mom is so crazy, it's no wonder that the precious offspring is also crazy." He found a bit of humor, but really couldn't understand why or how I could spend three hours with pasta and screeching women to gather my marketable facts. Are you kidding? I could trade this info like baseball cards with moms who hadn't been at the gab fest.

It's my job to get the dirt at the expense of Chianti. It's a hard job, but someone in the family has to do it.

-- Anne

This is no new news to you, but your reactions to change are a result of how you have programmed your brain computer. The good news is that you are not hardwired, and boosting your confidence during change requires nothing more than an increase in your self-awareness and a rewire of your point of view.

Early on, I am going to challenge you with listening to the squeak in your head. At first it might be nothing more than signposts of fear, or distressing over unknown outcomes. Eventually, I would like it to go a level deeper. I'd like it to probe a bit, describing fear of what, or loss of what, or insecurity with what?

And then eventually resound with the intentional and composed you.

EXERCISE

Where are you now?

Before you even begin to look at moving through this "something" that brought you to this book, take inventory of where you are.

If you are in the midst of a change right now, I want you to tell me what I would see if I were watching you. It's not like I'm a creep stalking you in your back yard, but close.

Describe your posture, figuratively and literally. How have your moods been? Irritable or fiercely focused? What about your level of energy? Feeling overwhelmed so you've taken to more napping? Stuff like that.

The objective of this exercise is to observe the situation as though you are an outsider. This will bring you the objectivity for starting the journey.

Write it here. The factors at play. The feelings. The unknowns.

I have provided several pages for you as a journal. I am going to call it the Journey Journal. I give you permission to write in this book. Think of me as your mother telling you it's okay.

By setting out with some introspection, you'll find that concepts that I present later in the book to have more context. It'll draw your attention to your reaction to your transition and hopefully change your perspective on it as well.

_____

_____

_____

_____

_____

_____

_____

_____

_____

_____

_____

_____

_____

_____

_____

_____

_____

_____

_____

_____

_____

2 WOMEN IN THE SPOTLIGHT

For women, the challenge of moving oneself through change may not be markedly more difficult than for men, but it is definitely different. Women see their worlds as an interdependence of many domains including work, family, community, and social. So when one area changes, it transgresses into the other areas. Transitions must be managed as a holistic project. Think of it as an outfit. Seemingly different parts of the ensemble need to ally with the others. You wouldn't grab just any belt without thinking through the shoe choice. Jeez.

About ten years ago I began looking at my training content for leadership and team-building from a woman's perspective. What would a woman like about this and that? How would I adjust the learning points for a group of women in a room, rather than a mixed population? If we are different in the ways of communicating, are we different in the way we prefer our training as well? And does that go for managing change too?

One problem with our self-development in the workplace is

that we have very few female role models. The consideration of a role model is hugely significant. When we think about the way something is done, we visualize it in our mind as being done by someone. With any luck, that imagined someone is an avatar of you, or a wanna-be. We call this a visualization, also a powerful tool for programming the mind to perform as if the vision were a reality.

And it works the other way as well …. it can work against us.

In your mind you are seeing the impending change in front of you as either an opportunity or you see it as an undertaking.

Seeing change as an opportunity

For those of you in this mindset, I applaud you. Your view of dental surgery is one that looks forward to the feel of periodontal intervention, or the discomfort of jaw pain. You don't see it as impending doom and a lockjaw that rivals the most uncomfortable pair of heels. Maybe you're craving the oxycodone. Maybe you step on ants for entertainment. I don't know, but you're a bit of an oddball. And that's a good thing, because it means you're likely the type that **leans into change with some positive energy.**

For you, the path to a transition with composure is only a matter of some serenity and self-management. We may need you to prop up the rest of us who are dragging our asses through the forthcoming doom.

Good for you. Keep it up. Whether it's natural or not, you are leaning into change.

Seeing change as an undertaking

However, if you see this change as an undertaking or something that is at least slightly dreadful, you're more normal. You may be fighting the demons of a past transition that was poorly executed, or you were the last to get chosen for the basketball exercise in gym class. It's probably something kinda deep but we won't get into anything like therapy here, so let go of that.

Here's where I will demystify those feeling for you.

There is a history of insecurity in women. The cause is directly linked to our position in the world. We are called "the fairer sex" but that doesn't get us anywhere, except maybe by the bouncer at Studio 54.

Being told as a young girl that you throw like a girl was an insult. Being outnumbered by men in your first post-college job taught you that you should do things the way everyone else was doing it, which happened to be the way a man did it. You were being taught the "norm," so you mostly wore blazers, the female version of the uniform of men, also referred to as the suit. They were all brown or black or dark blue. They projected professionalism! But we believe that makes about as much sense as leaving a lifelong career to suddenly become a colonoscopy nurse.

Suits project professionalism for men. Your industry may be entrenched in the penguin lookalike contest, but that doesn't mean you cannot look professional in a well-tailored skirt and blouse.

The point is that we sometimes become a victim to our surroundings. These pressures may result in you losing yourself and subsequently losing sight of your composure.

Your dread of change creates an albatross around your neck that is not nearly as flattering as the scarf you were eyeing in our virtual boutique. You HATE change. There I said it. If you don't HATE it, you dread it. Either way you just want to get through it faster and with more composure. You are so normal, and you are getting help – here. Keep reading

A little bit about your past and its authenticity

Besides discovering that no cosmetic product will ever reverse the aging process, what lessons have you learned from your past? I know that's a huge question and we'll give you some introspection space at the end of the chapter. So for now, think about what you'd call your authentic self? Think back to your early years either as a young woman or in early career positions. Would you say you were being yourself?

Consider what you now know as your authentic self. Your real self can be looked at in two ways, and in fact we want you to look at both. The "you" that is projected when you are most at ease and not threatened by negative forces like change in your life or gravity on your sagging bosom. And then the "you" that comes out in tense moments and periods of challenge.

Many women have a natural insecurity, and I would bet it has impressed upon you in some way, whether you are aware of it or not. You live in a man's world, which means you are a minority. Although it's not a doomsday outlook, it does have an effect on you. It may have impacted you in the past, and thereby it taught you to be on the lookout. Now, being faced with something that is pushing you through a transition, you are looking to what could go wrong, or what could hold you back.

Does that make sense to you?

We won't disassemble your past, but we will call upon you for insight.

But, aha, you are resilient.

The pressures in your past have also been the instruments that have tested you and made you stronger.

EXERCISE

As June would say, "Beave? Where have you been?"

Let's consider your personal situation, where you've been, and how you got here. I'll ask you to capture a little about your history.

This exercise is to capture what some of the ups and downs are that you have been through. No need to go into great detail here. Just write something that'll identify that period for you. I'll ask you to look for the bad and the good, the pits and the swells.

Pits = a down period in your life where you felt low, disappointed, or disoriented with the lack of progress or turn in your life or career. (hint: it's okay if now is one of them)

List several pits in your life by summarizing them here. Examples may sound like *The year my parents were divorced* or *Working for Emily at the firm*, or *The winter I spent on the Elm Street project* that you fondly call *the Nightmare on Elm Street*.

_____

_____

_____

_____

Swells = an era of happiness and contentment with your direction, feeling positive and secure with your situation. Examples may sound like *The early years at the 63rd Street house*, or *Running the assignment at Baker*, or *The summer I met Leanordo while studying in Spain and he taught me how to appreciate Paella and ancient ruins and topless beaches* and you get the picture.

_____

_____

_____

_____

_____

_____

_____

_____

_____

_____

_____

_____

_____

_____

_____

_____

This task is an exercise in increasing your awareness of present situations by qualifying your past situations. Take a look at those situations from a high-level point of view for a moment.

Now write a few words about each of the following:
What you have done well in stressful times, during the pits?

_____

_____

_____

_____

_____

_____

_____

_____

_____

_____

_____

_____

_____

What have you done well in easier times, during the swells?

_____

_____

_____

_____

_____

_____

_____

_____

_____

_____

_____

_____

_____

What gives you hope?

_____

_____

_____

_____

_____

_____

_____

_____

_____

_____

_____

_____

_____

_____

_____

_____

_____

As I take you into further chapters, you will begin to see the pits and swells as either an overstated or under exaggerated. Funny how that happens. Not haha funny. Odd funny. Therein will lie some connections to your strengths, and maybe your quirks too.

3 WHAT IS YOUR ROADMAP?

Since we are here, in part, to motivate and encourage you, let's paint a picture of a winning scenario – a woman taking on a change with self-awareness and composure. In this case, it's a woman named Julia, and she is in a tough work situation. For her, the stressful and critical environment is a constant challenge for her.

Whether your challenge is in your career or in your personal life, or you have the bonus of both, listen to the dealings of Julia's situation and the level of awareness that surfaces.

Our cameras focus in on Scene 1.

Julia's story was characteristic of the self-development hike that many of us take at certain times of our lives. She recognized her achievements thus far and the history that had driven her here, resulting in success. Nonetheless, she grappled with an undercurrent of feeling "stuck."

She couldn't name the roadblock. She just knew that there

was something that needed to be pushed through. Even reaching out to initiate something was met with an internal inertia, but she forced herself. She needed some sort of stimulus to uncover the nagging that was tugging at her, so she bargained with herself that she would just do something …. anything. Just start and figure out a direction later.

For her, the decision to get some professional development would be the tipping point she was looking for, so she signed up for a women's retreat over 2½ days in the foothills of the Southwestern desert.

This roadmap journey is a reflection of Julia, her workshop colleagues, and their collective experiences as they used the ROADMAP[1] to achieve clarity of a path forward.

ROADMAP is an acronym for a process to identify your journey as a story of yourself in progress.

Recognize Authorship of Your Change Story
Own Your Change Story
Assess The Storylines and Patterns
Decide What To Change
Map Changes
Author New Experiences
Program To Implement & Sustain Change

Recognize Authorship of Your Change Story

The backdrop of the Sangre de Cristo mountains was an appropriate setting for introducing this initial look at Julia's looming past and bringing it into focus. Julia saw her life as fundamentally good, but not necessarily evolving toward her most ideal future.

A group of women gathered for various personal and professional reasons, yet all were bound by a need to change something or work through a change that was happening to them.

From there, the energy flowed. There's something about an all-women group. Nothin' against them men, but barriers get dropped when it's just a girl gang in the room.

The group engaged in an initial exercise where they interacted verbally in a facilitated task to identify pits and swells of their pasts. They used each other as sounding boards as they reflected to one another, listening for verbiage may be connecting to an inner message. This was a time to increase awareness, whether one's past was intentional or not.

Own Your Change Story

As Julia heard herself speak, she also recognized the tendencies she exhibited to defer blame or "logical reasons" for a present behavior that was rooted in her past. Her newfound friends served to effectively patrol statements that they heard by jumping in with labels like "victim mentality" or "lack of self-worth." Raw, yet also surrounded by care and protection, and all interactions felt timely and well-meaning.

In fact, the entire group was mottled with interesting histories, some painful and others just misguided. Julia soaked in the openness and willingness of sharing the pasts … a parent that was absent or abusive …   the self-doubt that stemmed from being a female leader in a man's world … a series of unexceptional job assignments that developed into a lackluster career… an unfortunate childhood with too many conflicts.

In Julia's case, she owned the fact that she went through life unwittingly apologizing for nearly everything. She'd regularly start sentences with "I'm sorry to ask this but …" or reply to others with "Oh okay. Sorry." She asked herself why she would do this. She was not particularly meek, but she did feel something deep within her that was preventing complete confidence, something snagging.

Her realization was an understanding that she reacted emotionally to most situations, and got defensive or her feelings felt hurt. She was beginning to suspect that it was a deflection that stemmed from insecurity. She was insecure about what she brought to the table at her workplace so her emotion took over.

Julia was not recognizing the extent of the value she added, so consequently, she felt slightly inadequate. However, most of her co-workers would attest to her creativity, her resourcefulness in conflict, and her ability to move a group forward through a developing idea.   She definitely had something to add, but she was the last one to see it.

Without a firm grip of her abilities and embracing her self-worth, her future was likely to be unintentional. It was time to recognize that.

A Story of Initiating a Change

Want to talk about change?

I'll tell you about change… retirement. I started working in college and never really stopped until now. My biggest concern? My husband. He works from home and I was talking retirement and being at home, and he freaked.

My other concerns were, obvious – how do I retire? I had to assess the financial ramifications, discuss insurance options, tell my employer, finish my projects, and the biggest one of all – what comes next?

Planning a retirement is not for the faint of heart. It takes time to make the actual decision, anticipate the changes, plan out the exit strategy, answer everyone's questions regarding the "why" of retiring, consult a financial planner, calm your husband down, and then figure out what you are going to do when the alarm stops ringing in the morning.

For me, it was a year-long process. I had lots of conversations with family and friends, lots of change to consider and many soul-searching moments. But, in the end I knew it was time, physically, intellectually and emotionally.

What was it like? (I'm so glad you asked!) This change in my life was amazing because I planned it out. My employer was very gracious, and I gave them plenty of notice so there was no shock. My family was supportive, and I had plans for my afterlife.

How did I handle the changes in my lifestyle? By considering all of the options in advance – planning, visualizing, imagining, and talking about the changes. What are those changes? The alarm clock is silenced! Seriously, I can make my own schedule, I've made time for the things I didn't do enough of like exercising, shopping for healthy foods, traveling, etc. My husband has adjusted, my dogs have happily adjusted, and my kids get more attention and less stress from me.

Is change worth it? Absolutely. Embrace it. Work it. Tell your husband to call mine.

-- Anne

Assess The Storylines and Patterns

The women's next step was perhaps the most eye-opening, Through a structured process of visually mapping their past in a timeline format on a flipchart, each woman created a sort of pictorial of her story. The room was suddenly wallpapered with hand-drawn pits and swells, annotated by significant events and points in time that were meaningful. Some charts included artistic renditions of stages in life, colored with flowery achievements and communicating challenging phases.

During this time, Julia saw her past as a repeating pattern of making decisions based on an emotion that was triggered by others. Life directions were being driven by temporary and likely unintended reactions. She needed to face this head-on, by first recognizing it, then embracing it as a deep part of her and one that she had control over.

Then a funny thing happened. The conversation came around to a challenge of capturing the women's individual lifelines in a mantra – a one-liner that summarized the pattern that has molded you.

For Julia, it was frustrating because nothing surfaced that told her what her mantra might be. While she heard others create evocative taglines like "Transcend adversity," "It's time to move forward," or "Let it be," all with deep meanings for their own situation, Julia came up empty.

So she turned to Stephanie, the woman next to her, who had her own impression of Julia after a short day and a half. Through the clarity of someone else's eyes, Julia's mantra was summed up through Stephanie's ear, based on hearing her messages, themes, desired patterns, and true strengths. She said, "Julia, you're better than it."

And Julia saw what other's had been seeing for so long. The various *it* that came and went in her life that kept her from achieving a sense of accomplishment, and often a self-imposed barrier. She was better than the criticism she interpreted from colleagues, better than the negative self-talk that sent her into a blue mood, better than the tendency to lower her standards to accommodate others because she felt that boasting meant others would see her as arrogant or bitchy.

The *it* in the phrase was somewhat vague, yet held a deeper significance in reminding her of the power of her self. "I Am Better Than It" became her mantra.

Decide What To Change

With purpose comes clarity. Julia decided what she wanted. She would commit to see herself as an experienced and valuable member of her work team and not only look for what she added, but assume it was of value. She would practice setting aside emotional reactions and error on the side of action. She would be a tougher cookie by guiding her life with more intention and assertive communications. She would remind herself daily that power and fortitude do not equate to bitchiness or that she would lose friends over it.

She saw that there was an aspect of having more control in her direction than she ever thought she might. Once the indecisiveness lifted, the path became clear.

Map Changes

As the other women shared their journeys, the diverse directions cast an inspiring light on Julia's own outlook and more optimism emerged. Their strengths and courage in the face of various transitions showed Julia how much resilience there was in that room, and she was eager to move her life forward.

Julia's goals included a new commitment to stand up for herself, learn advocacy techniques, and practice a language that reflected self-confidence and a strong self-image. With some practice, she would more deeply listen in situations where difficult conversations may have otherwise triggered a sensitive reaction. She would turn those into productive interactions where her voice was heard.

What's important about experiences we go through are the lessons we learn and how we let them define us. Not only is change no different, but change can provide a defining moment!

Author New Experiences

Others would benefit from Julia's stronger identity. She would be a more influential role model for her ambitious children, her boss would appreciate an initiative that was backed up by a renewed self-confidence, and there would be a creativity that would emerge from feeling free of others criticisms.

Program To Implement & Sustain Change

Sustaining the new perspective was an important piece of the steps that followed. Julia feared that her optimism had only been a reflection of being among other strong women who also wanted to change.

Her newly adapted support mechanisms included daily practices such as a positive visualization moment each morning, and some communication techniques that reinforced her positive self-talk.

When she next saw herself in a compromising position, this time at work, Julia discovered that her outlook had completely changed. She had succeeded in letting go of previous reactions and didn't have to dig very far to find her voice, even though she new it was testing her. She stuck with it.

In one instance, Julia was facing a tough critic at work, someone she clashed with occasionally. It hadn't been an all-out conflicting relationship – simply one in which he was condescending to her and dismissive of her opinions. Before she would have felt inadequate. Now she pushed through. She was better than it.

Maybe all we ever need is an outlet, a setting to motivate us, and a ROADMAP.

1 - Krueger, D., (2009) *Live a New Life Story®: The Owner's Guide*, MentorPath Publications; www.MentorPath.com

EXERCISE

ROADMAP Application

For those readers who thrive with structured approaches, I would recommend the ROADMAP to track your progress (but don't stop taking your anxiety meds). Remember that moving through change is an evolution of growing, learning and reflecting. Understanding your uniqueness as a strength, not a liability, is a terrific start. If you'd like to extend the story metaphor, then see the ROADMAP as a way to label your past story as a byline to the future.

This space is intended to allow you to find the parallels in your own roadmap after reading Julia's experience. You will likely not be at the end of the seventh step in the process, but you may want to capture observations from any or all of the seven steps.

Recognize Authorship of Your Change Story

_____

_____

_____

_____

_____

_____

_____

_____

_____

_____

Own Your Change Story

_____

_____

_____

_____

_____

_____

_____

Assess The Storylines and Patterns

_____

_____

_____

_____

_____

_____

Decide What To Change

_____

_____

_____

_____

_____

_____

Map Changes

_____

_____

_____

_____

_____

_____

_____

Author New Experiences

_____

_____

_____

_____

_____

_____

_____

Program To Implement & Sustain Change

_____

_____

_____

_____

_____

_____

_____

EXERCISE

Visualization of an Intentional Future

This exercise is intended to put you in a frame of mind that transitions you from your past experiences into your present situation with intent and composure. Take the steps at a time when you can isolate yourself in a calm area, with the warmth of knowing you are alone with your best friend, you.

Take a moment to get in a quiet place where you have time for yourself. Get comfortable. Take a few deep breaths.

Then, read the following paragraphs as if you are coaching yourself and taking yourself through the process mentally, with your relaxed body obediently following.

Begin.

Picture your life as a continuum. Think about when you were born. I know you don't remember it, but imagine the room and your mother. What a change for her, a joyous, thrilling yet slightly disturbing change. And for you, this is where our journey of change begins. From the warm loving security of your mothers womb into the bright lights, loud sounds away from the viscous warmth you have known.

How do you suppose you must have handled it?

For some it's scary. For some an adventure. For all it's unknown.

Now move through the early years. Did you have certain sad or sorrowful times? Did you have happy and joyous times? Think about those times and how they built your character. The joyous times showed you could celebrate life. Looking back on the somber times gives you a sense you can move through suffering and emerge yourself again on the other side.

Now think about your adult life, you probably experienced a death of a loved one. Think about that and how it impacted you. You can look back with love and perspective that you did not have at the time. You are stronger and better for having known your loved one. You are stronger and better for having gone through all of the trials of your adult life. You are more empathetic, more courageous, more joyous in your zest because you move through whatever appears in front of you with ease.

Now think about the change you are facing. It is a challenge but you are able to face it and move through it with grace because you have done it before and you can do it again. Look at your ROADMAP find your strengths and use them through this brave transition.

4 ARE YOU AT A CROSSROADS?

Were you looking for that perfect silk scarf? Or did the scarf find you?

Seems it happens that way. It's not so much what we are looking for as what drops in our laps. Crossroads seem to be the same way. They appear.

There is a vast difference between change that we impose upon ourselves and those changes thrust upon us. A self-initiated change may be a reflection of a healthy view of constant change or a pain point reaching such a level of discomfort that you "just gotta move on."

Typical themes in a crossroads may look like:

> Biggies:
>> Divorce
>> New job
>> New career focus
>> New boss

New family
Taking care of parents
Empty nest
Financial difficulties
Breaking a detrimental habit
Serious injury or health issue

More subtle but still disruptive:
New project at work
Different work team
New IT system
Adjusted exercise routine
Different diet routine
Injury or new physical difficulty
Hormone replacement not working
Drinking for relief not working
Finding love online not working

Look those over and ask yourself which ones can be self-initiated before they are actually flung onto you. Go ahead and break up with the boyfriend before he breaks up with you. (You did NOT hear me say that. I was really just kidding.)

In this chapter's assignment, we will task you with assessing the change that is in front of you, or that you are moving through. With some introspection, you will start to grapple with your situation and how to best move yourself through it.

The high or low of a new change

Dopamine is the chemical in the brain that produces a feeling of pleasure. For those gamblers out there, it's the sense that runs through your brain when you walk into the casino with a handful of chips. Or the feeling of excitement that hypes you up when you decide to splurge on the milkshake, despite the likely belly ache later. (My sister calls that a Slumber Party Stomach and I remember them well).

We know from studies that the dopamine is released well before the actual event. In fact, it is delivered to our systems at the anticipation of a pleasurable event. We start feeling giddy before we have even put a single coin in the slot machine.

This may explain why the feeling of an anticipated event is a let-down. We enjoyed imagining it more than we enjoyed living it. You thought that new car would be a long-lasting thrill, but its excitement waned more quickly that you would have ever predicted.

That's the paradox of a positive event.

So, does the same concept apply for a dreaded event? Would you say your fear of the upcoming change was more sensationalized than the reality?

You bet! Along with the dreadedness (a word I made up) may come uncertainty, like the fear of skinny jeans looking like crap on you. We work it in our minds, work it, work it, sensationalize it. Now it's loomed in the back of our heads until it's as dreaded as a boil about to burst. You obsessor, you.

When do you force yourself to cross the road?

… and it's not "when you need to get to the chicken on the other side," although at some level perhaps it is.

If you've got that mountain in front of you, but you're hesitating, now is the time to check in with yourself.

This makes me think of Maria Von Trapp climbing every mountain and fording every stream, except it's me on a steep and snow-covered climb, and I have no boots on, and I'm wearing a bulky nun's habit, and it's a nightmare. It would be cool if a nun's habit could transform into a head-mounted jetpack. That would make a good sitcom. I wonder if anyone has ever thought of that.

Waking up to the grinding of teeth is a pathetic start to the day. Yet, many of us spend our nights filled with recurring dreams that are much less pleasant than the *Sound of Music*.

The underlying message … something needs to change.

Are there benefits to postponing change? In some cases, sure. A crisis fades or a situation alters in your favor. That's when I say "See! Procrastination pays." Yet living all parts of your life that way only leads to an unproductive series of stages for you.

Let's say your unbreakable pattern is to hit the snooze button a few times. If more than 50 times a morning, that may be an indication that you are avoiding something, wouldn't you say?

Other signposts of being in a rut:

You get hives driving into your employer's parking lot.
You come home at the end of the day and snap your spouse's head off when he says "hello."
You cringe when your boss asks for a few minutes of your time.

It might be time for a change. Okay, this kind of change is the big one. This is the one where you weigh (not on a scale): is it time for a new job? Is it time to retire? Is it time to ask for a raise?

The first question you need to pose to your un-made-up-face in the clear light of day is - what is the real problem here? Is it them, is it me, is it both? What's that pimple hovering like a land mine?

That's a lot of questions, but only **you** can sort out the answers. First, you have to get really honest with yourself.

This chapter is your time for addressing the crossroads you may be facing.

EXERCISE

Find a quiet place to rest your body and your mind. The farther away from the nagging pile of clothes in the laundry room the better.

Don't laugh at this exercise and stifle the need to giggle if you're in the room with your sister performing it.

Practice stilling your mind by taking a deep breath. Exhale it slowly. Repeat several breaths. I use the breaths as an analogy for a wave lapping into the shore, so I'll share that with you. Use the semblance of a beach with the in and out of the waves being like the in and out of your breathing. You are the water and your inhale pulls the wave out to sea from the seashore, like the air traveling into your mouth, deep into your lungs and distributed through your body.

Next, your exhale travels up onto the beach. The cyclic rhythm of the breaths mimics those of the waves in and out of the beach.

If you can perform this visualization without feeling like you are gagging on seawater, it's actually quite quelling.

Once you are settled into that relaxation, read to yourself the following grounding questions with your senses ready for your reaction. Pay attention to what your initial intuitive response is for each of the following.

I am aware of myself in this space and time.

I am aware that something needs to change for me right now.

I know the answer.

Did something become more clear to you? Did your intuition reveal anything?

Talk to yourself a bit here.

Thoughts, feelings, or conclusions:

_____

_____

_____

_____

_____

_____

5 CYCLES

There's a cycle that Mother Nature taught us. That's right ladies. That blessed cycle never seems to go away. For change, it is a little different. The repeating rhythm of up and down is more ubiquitous than you would suspect. Therein lies one of the little secrets about change and that is its predictable pattern.

I provided an exercise for you at the end of Chapter 2 where you were tasked with identifying the Pits and Swells in that rich history of yours. If you completed it, then you're tracking right along with me, my friend.

Putting that cycle to a series of named stages is the next step in understanding it. Akin to the five stages of loss and grief, transitions lead us through some damn-near predictable states. As you read through their descriptions, ask yourself how they have been verified in your own story.

Here are the four distinct states that indicate the cycle of change, à la Katie.

STATE 1 – STABILITY
Everything seemed to be going pretty well!

Let's be retro. Retrospective, that is.

Are you prone to nostalgia? Me too. It runs in my sappy family. So when I look back, I yearn for the seemingly idyllic times with warmth and aching. Of course you know the "good ol' days" punchline of living in the past. Those phases of life always seem sweeter in hindsight.

Consider, too, a career that has slowly progressed. It has not all been a walk in the park, but as you step back to survey the big picture, you've managed to achieve progress and earn experience, if only in little bits. It's all starting to add up.

I have finally decided that so many pieces of our path to the present may only look like stability in hindsight. If you are now in the throes of a change, then previous history may seem like a better situation than the present one. No matter .... stability is relative.

Whether you see a stable phase in your past as a far superior option to your present chaos or whether you sense that security has always eluded you, the lesson learned is to understand that present day may not be as unnerving as it feels.

Stability may seem like the place to be, but its inherent danger is complacency, possibly leading to lethargy. Ain't nobody got time for that.

Roller Coaster: Or, Don't Barf On Your Way Down

Ups and downs… we've all had 'em, whether in personal or professional situations, or both. Sometimes, an up and a down in rapid succession can feel like you are ready to get OFF of the roller coaster.

Recently, I had an awkward situation in my workplace that contained too many ups and downs, lots of emotion, and finally… a very clear moment of insight for me. As I volunteered to do an assignment that should have been taken by a co-worker (Fred said he didn't have time to do it, although it fell under his job responsibilities), it backfired on me. Fred's boss, Angela, accused me of trying to take away his work in a passive-aggressive fashion. But, she didn't say it to my face. She went to my boss and told her that I had acted inappropriately in offering to do Fred's job. HUH??

Really, I wasn't trying to be passive-anything. The task just needed to get done, and I had the time to do it.

But, here's what I learned. No matter your intention, sometimes other people will read the situation the way *they* want to. I have taken a term from Psychology and titled it *projection*. Angela projected her frustration at Fred not doing his job by calling me out. My boss didn't accurately interpret what he received, and told me I was in the wrong. HUH #2?

This particular shift in the dynamics of our work group actually caused me to stop and take stock. It wasn't the first time something like this had happened. I felt that the shift was too large for my comfort. This instance allowed me the GIFT of deciding for myself what I was willing to endure. It eventually led to my decision to retire.

Use the ups and downs. Position them in your own timeline... when have you had too many? What is bearable? What does an accumulation do to your stress level? Don't just endure them, use them as object lessons.

-- Anne

What is there to learn from the state of Stability?

My favorite answer … it depends.

It depends on you. Are you moved by a relaxing situation because it gives you the clarity to focus on other activities? Or do you need just a little tension in order to be creative? The rubber band analogy – you gotta have a little stretch in the rubber band for it to actually work well. Too much stretch, and it breaks. Stability may not be providing the creative stretch for you, but it is definitely a time to enjoy your undertakings and ride that train of life.

Let's move on to modern day life in the US of A.

STATE 2 – STRESS
Pressure to change in some way

I just finished an Amy Tan book about courtesans in early 20th century Shanghai and their stressful competition to remain young and entertaining. In addition to learning way too much about upper crust prostitutes and what a pudenda is, I came away with one quotation that reminds me that all life is stressful, even if all you do is twirl a parasol and sing ballads for Asian businessmen. Here's what one Courtesan Teahouse Madame stated:

"I must become a lady of leisure. Never hurried. Always calm. Maybe even a little lazy."

I especially liked the prospect of being more lazy.

During stress, your most exaggerated self may rear its ugly head. The reaction is different for each of us. We may initially find ourselves acting in a self-protective manner. In a way, we want to preserve the stability we just experienced.

In most cases, you just don't feel like yourself.

I could write an entire book about stress, and in fact have many tips about managing self and stress at the Skirt Strategies website. (www.SkirtStrategies.com)

For those of you in the audience with superpower capes, stress may be nothing more than recognizing it, embracing it, then letting it go. You are good at it. You self-manage well. Your diet seems impeccable and you'd never eat junk food. I am curious what you do when no one is looking because I am convinced that I can find FD&C Red Dye #40 under your fingernails from the Cheetos binge earlier in the day.

If you lack the spandex tights of a super-heroine, see the coping strategies in Chapter 8. I wonder if the word "heroin" is derived from "heroine" because it seems you'd need chemical supplements to achieve success during some demanding situations, but I would advocate for comfort food before recommending recreational street drugs.

This state called STRESS is marked by the transition from STABILITY to something not as appealing. You can feel it in your physical strain, mental worry, increased episodes of screaming in the car, or all of the above. It's staring you in the face, so time to cope, and move on.

STATE 3– SURVIVAL
Things get worse before they get better

In survival, a woman must accept that moving forward is, at this point, inescapable. Change or die: a compelling proposal.

Here's a small piece of calming advice in this stage of change, and it's not that resistance is futile, but that's a pretty good one. Don't sweat what feels like big stuff. Consider that it feels like a bigger deal than it is.

I once worked in an office where one of the guiding principles was "Err on the side of action." Misguided activity is a more welcome sight than no activity at all. Moving toward action will at least get your engine revved, then you can point it in the right direction. This concept is a part of why things get worse before they get better.

Here's a simplification of a business example. Consider a company that is seeing a flattening out in profits, or a business culture in a slow atrophy toward becoming a not-so-great-place-to-work. The stress of declining revenue or fading culture has created stress, and now the business is putting changes in place. Moving a workforce forward will disturb the status quo, interrupt existing methods in order to fix them, and usurp resources in the process. Previously complacent behaviors are now disrupted as they are called upon to try new work methods. Human resistance is marked by increased conflict, and a healthy rumor mill. You likely hear lots of "when I first started here, it was so different." Living in the past.

Fast Turnarounds Can Be Healthy

The cycle in our personal story can change direction in a heartbeat.

At one point I was sitting in my car after a James Taylor concert, contently gazing at the rain pouring across the windshield. My dominant thought was to get home and change into comfy jammies and relish the experience.

A blink later I was on a flight to another city ... someone needed me. Badly.

How does this change make you feel? Like you have jet lag, that's how. But this kind of quick-turn-around-change-of-plans actually makes for a more flexible you. You are rewarded with some endorphins for helping someone else. You were able to think your way through the logistics, and it worked! After all, the jammies will always be there.

Don't fear the ability you have to make a change, very quickly, for the good.

-- Anne

If your transition is a result of a business environment that has moved you into stress and survival, look first to yourself for sanity. Use the next three chapters to manage yourself, with the understanding that the environment around you may not be controllable, but your reactions to change are.

How about an example from the archive of a personal world? When I faced divorce in my early years of adulthood and with two children under the age of ten, I knew I was in the midst of my life pivoting, but I had no idea which direction it was headed. This shift in front of me was completely unknown, so I was simply surviving. A self-reinvention was necessary and figuring out the new me was trial and error. Things got worse before they got better.

For instance, to minimize the impact on the kids, my ex and I thought it would be terrific if they did not have to move to a new residence with me, so he offered the old house to me and the kids, rent free, for an indefinite amount of time. My ex would come stay with our daughters when I had a business trip. Seemingly easier for the children, but we tried it for a while and it was bad karma for me. Not gonna work. I had to move on and the space around me needed to change. Plus, the ex had a way of missing mortgage payments and all I needed was a surprise eviction from the bank.

For me, action led to ideas and a sense of progress. I moved into the new house, feverishly decorated kids' rooms, ordered accessories from Ebay, and figured out how to best manage my new schedule as a single mom. It was fabricated progress, but the feeling of advancing in anything was a mental reinforcement for me.

Adjusting to new routines during transitions takes energy and mental fortitude. Not all of them will emerge without snags. The mindset of assuming failure as a part of the picture is most vital here.

You will fail and still survive. The Macarena was a spontaneous creation that looked pretty stupid until the dance floor became a sea of poorly trained flamenco dancers. Then it really looked stupid. But line dancing went on despite it.

STATE 4 – the SHIFT
Starting to see a shift towards progress, feeling renewed

Your shift to a new phase is imminent, and your best bet for getting there is to accelerate the Stress and Survival states to get to the shift.

I left the safety of my engineering career to become an entrepreneur. Although a recruitment request by a national consulting firm was what wooed me into the transition, I knew it was where I would be happier in the long run. The stress was not necessarily difficult, but more like looking out through a foggy window into a nebulous future. Leaving stability automatically meant survival was at my doorstep.

When I put my first website together, there were NO easy tools because I was an early adopter. Wordpress did not exist. Most software was not free and shareware was unreliable. If you could find a WYSIWYG editor, it was rough and not user-friendly. Being a degreed engineer was what opened doors into learning HTML, and it nearly took the engineering credential to figure it out. I detested the burdensome process of writing, transforming, uploading, formatting, checking, researching keywords, blah blah blah. [Insert scream here]

To validate my evolution, I would toss around massive abbreviations like I just did with you. Hey, whatever works. Put me on that large-brain pedestal. Hope it worked.

I could have leveraged so much about the new internet world and made a fortune if I'd bought certain domain names like Leadership.com, Women.com, or more obtuse ones like Therapist.com, Bendover.com, Momsexchange.com or Speedofart.com (and who ever named it Pen Island? Extra points for putting that one into a URL and seeing what you get.)

But I knew that's where it was all heading so I jumped in. At some point I realized that I no longer hated social media or the nuisance of constantly feeling like my frequency of interacting was inadequate.

Your story is filled with chapters of these up's and down's, swells and pits, and indications of the four states of an ever-rotating cycle. Every once in a while you need to get off the tilt-a-whirl and let your stomach settle. I'd like to think that's what you're doing in this book.

EXERCISE

Find one of the pits chapters of your life from the exercise you completed at the end of Chapter 2. If you didn't do this exercise, enter the spank machine, and just think of a difficult transition you have completed sometime in your life.

Describe it here, including how you felt going through it.

_____

_____

_____

_____

_____

_____

_____

_____

_____

_____

_____

_____

_____

_____

_____

_____

_____

_____

_____

_____

_____

_____

_____

Assume I am your coach and I am giving you positive feedback for your progression through that stage. What are some of the reinforcing comments I would say to you about your behavior during that transition?

_____

_____

_____

_____

_____

_____

_____

_____

_____

_____

_____

If I catch you drifting into the "I was really bad at …" or "I hate that I did this and that …." then I'm putting that spank machine into double-speed-fanny-whack mode. I asked for positive feedback for yourself.

Extra consideration. As you look back at that transition, does it give you a sense of pride for having gone through it, regardless of whether you initiated it yourself or whether it was done to you? For example, did you get through a divorce with some sense of self-preservation and mild composure?

If so, then I am going out on a limb here … did you realize what a big transition it was at the time and yet you kept cool?

If your answer is yes, then you have earned yourself a cocktail and a toast to your accomplishment. That realization can have a calming effect on your present transition. After all, what you just admitted is that you went through a hefty change without really caving in, and you seem to have survived. Pain leads to growth.

6 REACTIONS: EFFECTS & RETORTS

When my traded-up version husband and I take my two daughters out for Italian, our first choice is the neighborhood joint for two reasons: it is truly authentic Italian and it's a family-owned restaurant. In fact, it was the first place that Sophie ate pasta as a small child. Ask me sometime about the time she sneezed a fettuccine noodle out her nose during dinner.

Luigi's must be the place for family experiences, because the most poignant example of how humans can have such an assortment of different reactions to the same stimulus occurred there as well.

Four people in a booth

A few years later my family and the two daughters, now as teenagers, were at Luigi's. We had just finished ordering when we heard a bodily noise from the booth next door. Now I'm not saying it was definitely something like a methane blast, but it sure sounded like it.

Here's the way each reacted to the gastric disturbance.

>Youngest daughter: "What was THAT?"
>Oldest daughter: "Ew. Gross!"
>Mother: Gasp! And embarrassment on behalf of the perpetrator.
>Father: "Oops, ex*cuse* me!"

The whole gamut … curiosity to disgust to shock to humor.

Our reactions to change are often a reflection of who we are and the situation at hand. We talk in the next chapter more deeply about better defining the loss in a transition, but for now we can safely say that most of us have responded in each of the various ways in various situations.

As you might learn from a good therapist or a trendy fortune cookie: how a change makes you *feel* is completely natural and should be accepted. It's how we see you *act* that is your choice and says the most about your character.

Reactions to change: a menu of options

I could probably label a woman's reaction to her transition based on her Facebook posts. I have one friend from high school that posts nothing but complaints about her life and her workmates. I won't be surprised if she has ordered her tombstone to read #stupiddumasscoworkers or #getthehelloffmyplanet or more likely #itoldyouiwassick. It's pretty sad.

Why is it that we are the last ones to hear what we broadcast to the world?

Behaviors, and misbehaviors, tell us so much about a woman's internal content. We are appalled when we see dramatic behavior in others, yet we sometimes find ourselves indulging in it.

Where do people really go when they are really reactive? Are you passive or aggressive, or worst yet, passive-aggressive?

Are you leaving the trail of bloodied bodies in your wake?

Watch yourself in your first tendency to react to change because it'll be a reflection of your most comfortable state.

Behavior: Accepting Change

Being accepting of change is one perspective of a reaction to change. It's a positive one, at least seemingly. You don't want to play the doormat all the time, or the "yes" woman, but you indeed may be a Pollyanna that jumps into change with ease.

In the mindset of Zen, it's pleasant to be accepting.

The philosophy of being willing to accept the things you cannot change can shine a light into the face that "resistance is futile." Sure it takes less energy in the short run anyway, and why not just give in?

Do you see yourself being accepting of change? If so, in what way?

_____

_____

_____

_____

_____

_____

_____

_____

Lessening The Drama: Or Drama Dealer Be Gone

Katie and I used to love being onstage! As you may have guessed, Katie was really good at it. We used every opportunity in our small high school to get on the stage and act/sing/play around, and get a few laughs or tears. We had wonderful mentors in our short stage careers, and those mentors taught us that drama has a place: the stage, not the classroom.

Well, the same is true for the workplace.

DO AWAY WITH THE DRAMA!

There, I said it. If you are guilty of stirring the drama pot, then stop. If you are guilty of being drawn in by some very strong personalities, then stop it. It's kind of like the old adage, "Nothing good happens after midnight." We want you to adopt a new adage, **"Nothing good happens when there is drama perpetuated in the workplace."**

Let's practice. Go ahead, we'll wait. Say it out loud.

Thank you! You have made one giant step towards an enlightened you. It may be the most simple, yet most important lesson of the day – or year.

- Don't deal in the currency of drama. It never ends up serving you or your reputation well.
- Drama usually revolves around subjective information, not substantive stuff. As a result, you may be labeled as a gossiper.

- Drama dealing is a time-sucker. You will be more productive and happier if you turn around and walk away from escalating drama. Even if it is just keeping your mouth closed in a heated discussion, play down the drama.
- In the end, hold your head high knowing that you did not cause pain or distress to anyone else by being a Drama Dealer.

-- Anne

Behavior: Resisting Change

A resistive reaction is occurring because, by golly, you care. You sense the loss. You're holding onto something that means something to you. You're making a point to yourself. You're being loyal to the old way or what you're leaving behind. No shame in that. But know that it is keeping you from moving on.

Resisting also may indicate your aversion to the risk in a new change.

When thongs were first introduced into the market, the previous term for flip-flops got dropped immediately. If grandma said she was going to K-Mart to get a pair of thongs, you immediately corrected her. Change is not always so good.

Have you actively joined The Resistance? Okay, you activist you, say more about what resistance looks like in you.

_____

_____

_____

_____

_____

_____

Behavior: Hiding Out

If you are the woman that hides out, you simply may not have the energy to take yourself through the stress and survival states. Maybe you have been burned and embarrassed. Maybe you have read on the internet that you should have your dream job. What the hell? That ship sailed when culottes and cowl neck sweaters were in style.

Hiding out is a self-preservation mechanism to avoid expending the effort to move on. A deep-seated philosophy may exist that it'll blow over or fate will prevail. Why engage if my actions won't matter?

Could you accuse yourself of hiding out? If so, what do you think is behind it? Why do you do it?

_____

_____

_____

_____

_____

_____

Behavior: Disassociation

"Whatever may be happening, it's not a good fit for me."
or
"Whatever may be happening, it's not of interest to me."

In fact, there may be a huge risk with the change, so divorcing yourself from it feels safe. You may be on the sidelines waiting for something to break loose or for the change to prove itself worthy of dragging you in, but for now, you prefer to have nothing to do with it.

Perhaps legitimately, your backing away is an indication of the issue not being a threat to your values, otherwise I would assume you'd have your sleeves rolled up and be ready to engage.

Maybe the new gas station that is planned in your neighborhood doesn't really sway you one way or another. Some people want the convenience of a nearby gas pump. Others strongly denounce it with environmental fervor. Your disassociation is a reflection that you have no skin in the game.

Remember, too, that disassociation may be a way to be uninvolved because you don't even know where to begin.

If you feel disengaged or disassociated, ask yourself what is behind it. Do you have energy but feel frustrated at such a depth that you don't know where to start? Is it a sadness? Describe it here:

_____

_____

_____

_____

_____

_____

_____

_____

Behavior: Acting out

Here you are and you DO know where to begin, so we are hearing from you, for sure.

"I'm pissed and you're all going down with me."

Acting out in change is the outward manifestation of the energy within. Beware, dear reader, if you find yourself acting out. It can be a quick road to attacking others and thereby compromising or even severing some relationships.

My interpersonal style is expressive, and with that style comes outbursts and blunt vomiting of unfiltered junk.

The human brain does not think logically when in the throes of an emotional surge. Instead, we are thinking with the amygdala, located in the sub-cortex of our brains and the part that correlates to aggression. It is often triggered by fear. What does that tell you?

When the amygdala is engaged, it hijacks the prefrontal cortex of the brain, essentially bypassing your logic and clear-headed thinking. Avoiding an amygdala hijack will help you to keep your cool.

For many of us, avoiding an emotional outburst is a big challenge.

I, and probably many of you, have learned that if you just give something 90 seconds of thought, it will deflate the aggravation immensely. That's it, just 90 seconds of not reacting and actively breathing will help diffuse some situations. My road rage has considerably lessened. Just sayin'.

What humbles me most about acting out is the necessity to be a mature adult and return to the scene of the crime later with a heartfelt apology. Ugh, if you know the feeling, you know it'd be better to learn how to best control the original flare-up.

How much do you have the tendency for acting out when faced with change? Does it come from a fear? If so, can you articulate that fear?

_____

_____

_____

_____

_____

_____

_____

_____

_____

Change You Thought You Wanted

"You had better change your attitude, missy!"

Wow, how many times did you hear that one growing up? How many times have you said it to your own kids? I swore I wouldn't say to my children what my parents said to me. Ha!

Some *change* - although well intended - is not as realistic as we might expect. And, as it turns out, maybe I didn't really want that amount of *change*, after all.

It ended up being useful phrase, that one. I used it for the "missy" and the "master" But, here's the thing... the more things change, the more they stay the same. Parents need tools to raise children. Those tools really don't *change* through time, even if hairstyles and cell phone chargers do.

-- Anne

EXERCISE

What's your behavior right now?

If I am your closest friend, near you a great deal, and beside you as you make this transition what would I see in your Facebook posts as your hashtags? That's a sure way of asking for the trends in your actions, whether acting out, hiding out, or opting out.

_____

_____

_____

_____

_____

_____

_____

_____

KATIE K. SNAPP

7 LOSS – (YOU WILL) DEAL WITH IT

See that door? Notice that it's a little ajar (it's a door too). That's your proverbial opportunity for moving forward, and the name on the door is "LOSS." Translating loss as an opportunity is a mature way of finding a path through transition.

The loss we talk about here is one that is indicated by not moving forward. If your loss is a more serious one, such as your old husband Elmer dying or your fight with Leukemia, please also look for professional support.

For now, consider a more manageable loss you may have in a career that changes, or a life change like an empty nest, or a health issue that's affected your lifestyle. Fill in the blank with *your* transition or loss. Let's see if I can help you lighten up some of the losses and make them less cumbersome for you.

Career situation first: was there something about your job that was eliminated, or perhaps your complete job was axed? Let's say your job just changed … whether through your initiation or not by choice. Think of the loss as what you just gave up. For example, you were great at networking in that industry. Or you had a terrific team built. Or you created the last big successful marketing campaign, and you won't be around to live it out. My heart goes out to you, but I also know you can get through it. Start with the articulation of what you lost. And you have to do it without whining or at least without whining publicly.

Personal situation: the kids are out of the house and it's an empty nest. If you're seeing that as a loss, then I don't get you. But okay, it is the end of an era. I think I whined for about four minutes. It's not so much that they were difficult, it's that I love my time alone. I know it devastated some women. I really do get it.

Let's try another one. Divorce. It can painful on many levels, and can shake your self-confidence. You may feel like a failure because you didn't stick with it longer or devote yourself like Laura Petrie then or Olivia Pope now. You wonder if you quit too soon, then you hear something incriminating about him through the grapevine and you're validated again.

Regardless of your situation, take a look at what seems to be preventing you from moving forward. This may be the loss of a person, or loss of position, or loss of a future, or loss of security.

Here's a challenge for you. Adjust your perspective from fear of the future, to comfort of the past.

Let me explain.

We often categorize our resistance to change as an opposition to facing an unknown future. Some things you may hear yourself say -

"It's not that I mind change. It's that I don't like adjusting to something new that's more stupid than before."

"I'm worried about leaving a situation that I had worked so hard for."

"I'm great at accepting change," – stated by the person you know to be the biggest complainer when something changes.

The forerunner to your adjusting to change is your initial gut reaction to it. Something that you noodle on, often subconsciously. In fact, it is the loss.

It's an advanced concept, and one that requires a bit more emotional intelligence. I give women the nod on being better at emotion intelligence. This capability leads women to being more self-aware, and thereby more likely to explore their pasts or what is going on inside their behaviors. Women are more prone to dig into each others' loss with an empathetic ear and often some helpful explanation.

Revisit the most recent girls' night you experienced. For me, we sat on my throw-pillowed patio furniture set and gabbed. Sure, there was some wine. "Some" is a subjective term so I am fine using it. We were the perfect picture of the Pier One catalog. I felt so accomplished.

Here's a conversational lineup that illustrates how well we

manage each others' losses, pasts, and provide empathetic needs to each other:

"I have no idea what to suggest for our next book club assignment. Has anyone read anything lately that they love?"

The Goldfinch was great, but it was long."

"I can do long books now that I listen to everything on audio. In fact, when I am in a good one, I take off on a long walk just to catch up on the plot. So it's helped my fitness."

"I think Jodi Picoult's new novel was just released. Can someone pull it up on their iPhone? Let's get a description."

"Did you see the 50 Shades movie? Whatever happened to the movie night we were planning?"

"Gawd, Pamela, you look great in that skirt. Are you losing weight?"

"Had to! That last test I had done gave me a scare with heart disease and it runs in my family."

"How are you doing it?"

"Just better eating and lots of cardio. The FitBit has opened my eyes to how active I really am. I wear it all the time."

"But Pam, I have never been to an event where you weren't at the center of it all and running around like a wild woman!

You are in charge of everything and put so much effort into it! You've got great endurance!"

"I know. It's cray cray. I just need to stay focused on improving my health or else I'll have to give up all those events. They're making my hair fall out."

"It's hard but you can definitely do it. And who cares if we all aren't as skinny as Jennifer. We just need to be active enough to get around easily and stay mobile. I hope your next heart test comes out better."

"Thanks. I've had to give up the extra committee assignment at the club. It was just too stressful and I decided to pull back on some things. It's just not worth it."

"I know. Me too. By the way, did your mom enjoy seeing *Wicked* when she was in town?"

"Yes, and it was great to spend time with her alone since dad died. We are trying to find a new rhythm for our own time together without lapsing into anything too sad from the past."

"It'll be hard to adjust for a while, but you may want to look at it as the start of your own time together to celebrate how you both loved being around your dad. It'll help to talk a little about it, but then make sure you keep her from getting too weepy. I think that makes her more sad."

BTW -now's the time to pull out that "Would a man even say any of these same words?" card.

That's the illustration of the emotional intelligence at play between women, and it's a GOOD thing. It's communication on a different level and no hesitation to give each other compliments, ideas, empathy, and supportive advice to get through a loss or an adjustment to something new like a lifestyle change or health issue.

Talking with others brings out awareness. I will go so far as to say that if you are more aware, you are more likely to adapt to any change, and more importantly, you'll recognize whatever the loss is at the heart of it.

That's where the progressive thinking is involved. A self-aware woman will see her resistance as a sign of a loss. She will delve into questions about how her resistance is sprouted from the fear of losing something.

Let me repeat part of that ... A self-aware woman will see her resistance as a sign of a loss.

Loss is the key indicator of what may be holding you back.

Let's say that your transition is your being on the edge of a career change, or even retirement. The looming future may be appetizing but scary. Why wouldn't you simply jump into it like the way you'd stampede toward the new Lululemon outlet? Why? Because you are giving up something now. That's your resistance – the fear of that loss.

Empathy in Action

One of my former bosses always said, "What do you think? What is your advice?"

At first, I thought she was kidding. You're asking me?? But, not only was she asking, but she was also listening.

After an exchange between us, she would come back days later and tell me that she had thought about our conversation, and that she had done something that I said or suggested, and it had made a difference for her. It was the most amazing endorsement of my ideas and skills.

Imagine doing that for someone else. That's your job here, think of that.

-- Anne

Begin with an inventory of what made you comfortable in the present or recent past situation. Maybe there was a stability with it. Perhaps a consistent income, or a reassurance that you were good at something. Naming it is critical. The exercise in this chapter will lead you through that.

Many women see a loss when they see change. Leaving a career that may have been at its pinnacle.

Pain leads to growth.

Extra credit reading for my cerebral readers: Emotional maturity is often referred to as Emotional Intelligence (EI) or Emotional Quotient (EQ). EQ is to feelings as IQ is to intellect. It was coined by Daniel Goleman, who identifies five skill sets or main elements of EI, detailed as follows.

Self-Awareness – Knowing what's going on inside of your own head. Being aware of your mental posture, mood, preferences, and intuitions.

Self-Regulation – Managing all those moods and tendencies. Keeping control of your impulses. (My tell-all for this one is how I feel when I wake up the next day after a tense meeting or a lively social event. How saddled am I with the unsure feeling that what I said may not have been diplomatic.)

Motivation – Emotional tendencies that lead you to get what you want. Motivation is what gives you the initiative to move forward, especially in the face of barriers, challenges, and other setbacks.

Empathy – An empathetic female leader is aware of how others are feeling and what they need. You are good at putting yourself in others' shoes and connecting to them through an empathetic perspective, even if you disagree with their sentiments. You'll see empathy mentioned in the Coping Strategies chapter.

Social Skills – You're good at workin' the crowd, baby! And that includes one-on-one relationships as well. When emotions are in play, you handle them, being responsive to the social cues that you read, especially when mediating may be required.

I find all of these factors to be absolutely *amazing* and so revealing of how we can better manage ourselves and get what we want! I highly recommend any of Goleman's books.

Reference: Goleman, Daniel. (2006). *Working with Emotional Intelligence*. New York: Bantam Dell.

Specific Help for Job Changers:
Typical Elements of Loss

When the change has to do with your job, consider your options. What may seem like a looming and difficult decision may break down to identifying the factors.

Because Anne had been through a few job jumps, I asked her to contribute what she would perceive as the down-and-dirty list of the real issues. Here are her answers:

Income

Must you have it? Can you do with less? Mostly, income is a reflection of a sliding scale that begins with a minimal level for survival. This Maslow-like concept takes on a different value once you cross over from "minimal amount needed to comfortably live" to any higher level.

Health Insurance

You can't live without it. It's complicated out there so I urge you to find a friendly resource who can help you navigate this one.

Self-fulfillment

Yes, it's this important to be #3 in the list. It might be why you are getting the hives in the first place. If you've always wanted to pet short-haired dogs for a living, then find the best non-profit shelter you can. Volunteer, apply for a job, make yourself indispensable. Dig within yourself to find your source of fulfillment.

Standard of living

Yes, Princess, the style to which you've become accustomed. Do you really need that much of a car payment? Do you need all the stuff? Get rid of some stuff. You may find it liberating.

Your location

Are you in the right place? Hate cold weather and live in Minneapolis (No hate mail, please - I love Minneapolis!), then make a change. People really do feel better when they are in the right climate. The cost of living makes a big difference, too.

Your family and friends

Take this one seriously. You might need to get away from some family. Or, you might need to keep the friends you call family very close to you. Don't change your entire existence until you think about these people. They ARE your people, after all.

Your value

Do you deserve more? We saved the last for really poking the hornet's nest. Women are notorious for undervaluing themselves and we don't want you to fall into that same trap. Remember that your experience and what you bring to the table may feel like less of a contribution because you have been living so close to it. Err on the side of aiming high for yourself.

Don't get frustrated if this takes more than ten minutes to sort out. Take time, but listen to what your heart says. Sometimes we can overthink decisions. Talk to your gut.

EXERCISE

Assume the position. That is, assume you are in a position where you have made the decision to move forward and you are ready to let go of the aching resistance. I want you to define that resistance and what loss it represents.

What are you leaving behind? What have you accomplished that you feel you are giving up? How would you describe the loss?

_____

_____

_____

_____

_____

_____

_____

_____

_____

_____

Now, with the loss being defined, is there a way you can replace or replicate that loss to fill its absence?

For example, is your loss was the comfort of using your expertise in the old job, consider what you also do well that you can put into play. If your loss was a role as an active mother, and now the kids are out of the house, where can you go to stay active and provide support for others, such as volunteer work? Ideas here.

_____

_____

_____

_____

_____

_____

_____

_____

8 COPING STRATEGIES

My husband and I recently heard this quote from gentleman friend who was talking about his enduring career.

"It's doesn't get any easier. But it does get better."

To which I observed, "Kinda like marriage."

To which my husband inserted something about my being his third wife. I would have taken it as a compliment except I think he was inferring that his next wife would be better.

Coping is a very personal choice. The factors involved include:

> The impact of the change
> The depth of the loss
> The irreplaceability of the loss
> The length that the "old way" endured
> The potential for the future
> Your own resilience

Your ability to self-manage or the lack of it

The ability for those around you to self-manage or the lack of it

My guess is that you have some pretty good coping mechanisms already built into your tool kit. Since we women prefer hauling a Chanel purse of scavenger hunt must-have's over a kit of Craftsman tools, we are going to call our Kit Bag a Cosmetic Bag. (There's a joke in there about a wench, but I'll let you write it yourself).

Your objective is to acknowledge what you use naturally from that bag and what you'd like to implement more. Awareness is critical, for those actions that we do not implement as intentional, we leave to fate. In other words, start paying attention to your actual behavior, Little Missy, because most of us don't actually do everything we really wish we did. Emotions can get the best of us, and lack of keen self-management is rampant in our topsy-turvy world.

Professional as well as personal development requires directing a spotlight on our behaviors, something that can be humbling or even humiliating, but critical for growth.

Bigger change. Bigger disruption.

Do you agree?

The Timeline For Coping

My husband is German, I am American. My husband is an engineer, I am not. So, when we got married (after meeting on an airplane!), I told him that I am already two languages behind. I don't speak German or the Geek Speak of engineer-ese.

Almost 25 years later, I'm still trying to figure out what he's saying.

We are each very capable people in our own rights, and I keep telling myself that. But, get a verbal crossfire going across the kitchen table about how the router for the internet in our house works, and it's downright comical. He can't understand that I can't understand his complete gibberish regarding the technical merits of a box that communicates through our living room furniture.

Perhaps the vast change that I experienced as a new wife so many years ago is still in the coping phase. That does not sound like a promising outlook for my future, but I would propose that our communication is an ever-evolving change.

After nearly 3 decades with my techno-chatter husband, I have finally learned that his explanations begin in the middle of a story. He assumes I am well-versed in all the basics (wrong...) and that I had read the first two chapters (double-wrong ...), and so he is launching into the third chapter of the users manual on the gadget that I didn't know or like.

I finally coped. Call me a slow learner. I changed my approach. Now, I put him in reverse and back him up to the table of contents in ANY discussion we're having, and my big-picture brain gets it! Well, almost gets it, unless he's speaking in German to me.

There is no timeline for coping.

--Anne

I would confess that it's more of "different" disruption, versus a bigger one. It probably requires more planning and some coping strategies.

The following coping strategies are options for you to consider in your transition.

Coping Strategy: The Bridge of Planned Uncertainty

In corporate change, it's not unusual for a newly implemented system to be thrust upon its victims. Does this sound familiar to you? Raise your hand if you have been amid a software upgrade that left a trail of casualties in its wake?

If so, then let me guess -- the IT department formed a dysfunctional geek squad team to upgrade a critical business system using a cursory discovery phase with the users, using an implementation strategy that seemed completely logical from the back-end control room.

Major developments in a workplace take a carefully planned approach, weeks or months of planning, and a balanced execution using loads of stakeholder feedback and a capability to fluidly implement lessons learned. If it makes you feel better, no one does it very well. I could probably make a fortune forming support groups.

But one simple approach that can take some risk out of the implementation is the **bridge**.

In the bridge approach, a transition is implemented in at least

3 phases with a built-in stage for designed chaos. Try this on if it fits your situation.

Stage 1 of the Bridge: The Old Way

This is your situation before the change. The most valuable activity during this phase is to inventory what ideal outcomes you would like and what is presently working well. Although this exercise may foster some "don't touch my stuff" mentalities, those old way elements are important to acknowledge for two reasons. First, if they are invaluable, they need to be labeled so that they can be reproduced in some way in the new system. Kinda like the "I am the Blackberry expert around here. Sorry, Sista, that phone is going the way of the turtleneck dickies. Secondly, they must be identified so that they can be let go if they are not existent in the new system.

Stage 2 of the Bridge: Planned Uncertainty

In recent years, I have noticed implemented changes where a company was deadset on getting something up and running, right the first time, and everyone on board. Righto Chief!

Although there is some value to a kick start, I contend that we miss an opportunity to go slow so that we can go fast later. Enter the bridge phase.

An intermediate phase, with a planned beginning and end, and its own unique objective. Its purpose is to plan for, maybe even design, and then "try on" the new change with a mindset of taking in lessons learned and being open to tweaks and adjustments.

This phase works well when you need a pilot phase, but it works as well for the IT implementation as it does for the "new way of living" or eventuality in the "new job."

Lindley is a great example. She is the marketing expert in the company. Oh wait … she *used* to be the expert, until it grew into a different animal. The company either looked completely different than when she originally started there, or she has been fooling herself into thinking it was something else from the beginning. Married under false pretenses. Like a tempting dating profile on EasyDate.com that whispered all the right things, then proved to be a dud once you got to know him.

Knowing that she was headed somewhere else, Lindley saw change on the horizon but couldn't stomach the fear of a big leap.

When Lindley went through this process of coping, she started with a clear definition of what she *used* to be, or was about to leave behind. Sounds a little sadistic, I know. But it's useful for the reasons mentioned in the "Old Way" paragraph above.

Next came the definition of the bridge. For Lindley, she defined it as the six months between making the decision to change jobs, and being settled into the new one. This bridge included, by design, the tentativeness of giving notice for leaving her job, the actual deed of giving notice, working with a coach on her strengths, an upgraded résumé, and accepting a period of feeling ambiguity … *planned* ambiguity. This all-inclusive phase was six months, but that interval was arbitrary.

It could have been shorter or longer and filled with loads of other calming events, like a professional development class or a cheap cruise to a tropical destination. That's the beauty in it. It's designed by you. The result? A feeling of being in control, despite the circumstances. Brilliant.

Stage 3 of the Bridge: The New Way

Although the three stages of the Bridge to Planned Uncertainty applies nicely to the fouled up business plan, it also can have great application in a personal situation.

For example, let's say Marisol is distraught over the last of her three children leaving the house for college in the Fall. She prided herself on being the go-to mom for all of her children and their friends, especially the ones from households with less-stocked refrigerators. No more high school soccer games or school events. It's the end of a chapter.

For Marisol, the upcoming adjustment was dreaded. In fact, the more she thought about it, the more it saddened her.

The physiological reaction in the brain during the anticipation of an event can be more powerful than the actual event. For us girlies, that translates to "the expectation of the upcoming annual pap smear can be worse than the actual event." In hindsight (no pun intended there), it wasn't really all that bad.

In Marisol's case, I would coach her to identify a Planned Uncertainty phase either before the kids flew the coop or right after it happened. No need for cold turkey. Here are two possible options for a case like this one.

Option 1 – Spend the three weeks before the start of college acting as if the kids were already gone, but nearby. What would be your new routine for dinners, entertainment, interaction with family members? Use this intermediate phase to adjust to the new life while still knowing at some level that the kids were nearby. Get a little dose of them as you need it. Ask yourself what you miss about the old way, and what you love about your new independence.

As a humorous aside, kids have a way of getting under your skin right before they leave for college. It's part of the natural selection of moving out. Make mom mad enough and she'll forget she was going to be upset!

Option 2 – Spend the three weeks after they leave in a planned phase of grief and subsequent rebirth. Talk about the pros and cons of the new life coming up for you … the freedom, time to yourself, the security of the future now that the kids are on their own. What is your new daily schedule? And, allow yourself some time to grieve, if that's how you feel. A weekend away with the hubby in different environs often helps soften the blow. Picking someplace scenic with massages also helps.

Does this coping strategy work for you? If so, how might you capture the old, the bridge, and the new? This might take some creating.

Coping at Work

Why, for the love of all things sane, would department A make a decision for department B, when department C needs to implement it? Sounds theoretical? Think again. Names have been changed to protect the innocent, so don't try to pin this on your co-workers. But, then again, it could be your workplace, right?

Typical Scenario:

A: You need this new system, B. It will make you faster and stronger and your boss will love you.

B: Okay, how much does it cost and who does the work?

A: Oh, it's cheap, you can afford it. Guess what, C does the work!

B: Great, buy it, we'll try it.

C: What the heck is this and how am I supposed to use it?

B: Ask A.

A: Ask B.

C: Sigh.

True story, and it happens all of the time. In most cases, we'll find lots of blame-throwing, secret emails, clandestine conferences, and no real answers. In most cases, you... my dear woman, are C. It takes some real coping skills and some self-confidence (which you will have from reading this book) to deal with the situation.

-- Anne

Coping Strategy: Tough Skin

My friend Caroline has the toughest skin of anyone I know. She battled breast cancer, a double mastectomy, emergency hysterectomy, and West Nile Virus, all in a three-year span. None of those were choices. Each was thrust upon her.

My mentor coach, David Krueger states it this way, "It's not so much what happens to us, as what we make of what happens to us."

Caroline was heroic and composed through it all, but she was tough before that chapter in her life. She would even call herself insensitive, something that I observe with a bit of awe, because it absolutely works for her.

The ability to set aside an emotional reaction is an incredible asset. It allows us to think with our pre-frontal cortex rather than with the reactive brain (called the amygdala but I didn't want to sound too erudite and edumacated).

I learned tough skin early in my consulting career when my colleagues were bantering one evening with some collegial mocking, and I jumped right in. When I became the subject of a playful tease, I took it personally and was immediately offended. I am sure it showed on my face. One of them stated, "Katie can dish it out but she can't take it." Oh jeez that hurt. And ... he was completely right. What a weak dufus I felt like. Everyone else was not only taking it, but also razzing right back, in fun and funny fashion.

You're likely still going to run into the insensitive dolt out there, or the acerbic woman with a sharp tongue. Not every comment is intended in a harmless way. Rise above it. Picture yourself as the composed recipient that appears unruffled. People can be cruel. It's almost always about them and some hefty baggage.

Tough skin in a transition situation will get you to the next phase more quickly. If, on the other hand, you wear your heart on your sleeves — as some of us do, being tough-skinned is a learned and practiced art. It is hard work. Being a softy can be lovely at times, but it can also be your worst enemy in the workplace. Just be conscious of your own poker face… are you an open book or can you conceal some of the emotions?

Do you have tough skin? If not, how might this coping strategy help you through this transition? What would you like to do to toughen up that dermis of yours?

_____

_____

_____

_____

_____

Coping Strategy: Embracing Loss

We can thank Sheryl Sandberg for starting (or at least prolonging) the popularity of the phrase "Lean in," and I have found it a metaphorically useful term.

Its helpfulness makes complete sense to me. In change, we may resist, so the natural reaction is to hold back. Leaning in sends the message of pushing yourself into provoking some sort of action. In fact, don't even think about what the action may be. Just start the mental process of facing the loss, head-on. Visualize the loss your arms actually hugging what you are letting go. That's it. Bear hug. Send those sweet little babies off to college. Push them out the door after making a dramatic scene of maudlin weeps and gasps. Sometimes you can literally view "leaning in" as leaning toward someone to listen closer, as if you had trouble hearing them. Lean toward your own inner thoughts and gut feelings.

For you risk-avoiders, I can feel your body tense and lips purse at the thought of just doing something without knowing the outcome. Okay fine. Find another strategy, but I tell you this will get you out of that funk. You've been standing on the side of the pool full of anxiety and fear of the unknown temperature. Once you've plunged, the initial shock may spank you, but you'll grow accustomed soon.

Does the embracing or "lean in" approach fit you? If so, ask yourself what the mental equivalent of jumping in the pool would be. What would you say to yourself to move forward in that way? Actually write it down here, then say it out loud.

_____

_____

_____

_____

_____

_____

_____

_____

_____

_____

_____

_____

Coping Strategy: Letting it Go

My favorite spa resort is Miraval in Tucson. Throughout the 11 years that my sister and I have been going there we have been in various phases of personal need or domestic drama, from family illness to wardrobe malfunctions in public, to ex-husbands making a spectacle. Each trip feels different and from each we have left with some level of enhanced awareness and subsequent self-development.

Miraval embraces the Life in Balance byline that Kara and I so enjoy, but for more reasons than you may initially think. For one, make your own choices as to what balance means in your own life, because you are more likely to commit to them (duh). But for another, life should balance restraint with indulgence.

Enter Miraval's full bar. It is unlike other discipline-based spas where we believe that silly "dry" policy completely backfires. Might as well call it "pay for suffering." No lesson learned there!

But of all the little lessons that I have learned from the trainers and nutritionists and woo-woo speakers at Miraval, one particular lesson from a Yogi there stuck with me, and has stuck since then.

During a meditation class led by Mary Grace at the Agave Yoga Center, several of us sat comfortably in a circle on floor pads staring at a series of gong bells. (I know they are not called gong bells, so sorry if I have just offended anyone).

The Agave Yoga Center is situated at one end of the

property close to a somewhat busy street, so you can hear the occasional car whizzing by if the windows are open.

"Squirrel!" is my middle name, so imagine Katie in a meditation class with any sort of distraction. As if reading my mind, the yogi mentioned the auditory intrusion of the traffic and took us through a brief instruction to manage it.

"As you find yourself peaceful and physically relaxed, quiet your mind by stilling your thoughts. If you find yourself disturbed by outside stimuli, like the traffic, simply listen to it, embrace it, and accept it as 'the way it is.' Then let it go. Visually releasing it."

So simple! And so perfect for the follow-on to the embracing strategy.

Those of you familiar with any Buddhist teachings will recognize the "accept the now" philosophy here. Not to bring religion into this, but there are several well-known writers and philosophers (Eckhart Tolle, among them) who talk much about being present in the moment. Just some food for thought...

By resisting change, we actually embrace it. We are inviting it into our thoughts.

From my husband comes "Jeez, the neighbors blower is really loud, as loud as a commercial one. That's irritating! Is it just me?" Answer, "well it *had* been just you, until you drew my attention to it." Then it drove me batty.

The mental task of letting go may be an advanced approach, but with persistence, you can master it.

Is this a coping strategy that may benefit you? How might you try the letting it go approach?

_____

_____

_____

_____

_____

_____

_____

_____

_____

_____

Coping Strategy: Making it Simple

My newly updated version of Quickbooks is a piece of crap. It has constantly led me into an abyss of stupid mistakes and hours of unproductive fixing and reloading. There have been times where I sit at my desk frustrated to tears.

I'll give Quickbooks a slight break here. The original software was not make to run on a Mac and I am as hopelessly devoted to my iMac desktop as Olivia Newton John is to John Travolta. To complicate things, I cannot bear the thought of switching my software over to something else (how's that for resisting change? I preach this stuff ... I don't actually DO it. Just kidding!)

So here in front of me lies a big hairy mess of financial junk, needing a monthly reconcile and lots of tweaks and fixes.

I can't stand the thought of it. But I know I must. I must reconcile the books.

My dad used to use the word "simpleton" to call out an idiot. Now I want to be one. To see something as a simple and manageable task I elevate myself up to the 30,000 foot level. I once dated a pilot, but the analogy doesn't come from there. A high-level flyby is as uplifting as a fine-looking flyboy. Oops, did I say that? Silly. I meant as uplifting as a breath of fresh air after a crowded hot yoga class.

By starting with a high-level view, you are led to see the starting point and desired outcomes of a weighty task.

Here's one story of a woman grappling with a flattened career. Say how we will take her seemingly complex situation by taking what feels like a weighty decision and breaking it into small simple sections.

Annie doesn't know how she got stuck in corporate America, but there she was, mid-30's, tech-savvy and underutilized. She floated through the company, enduring organizational changes that inadvertently affected her and thoughtlessly changed her upward ladder. Perhaps the most frustrating was the lack of appreciation she received from her direct boss. She seemed to be drifting.

When she came to me as her coach, all she knew was that she was stuck. It looked like hairy dilemma of having been railroaded into a career where she was lost in a big company. So we started at the big picture and simplified it. We kept it at the issue of "career change" and nothing more. That made it digestible without all the dreaded thoughts of "what about benefits?" and "who would hire me?" We would ease into the details as they emerged.

A productive step in simplifying is to <u>begin with what you know</u>. Gather the data that presently exists. Draw upon irrefutable facts of your situation, such as how you feel or what is nagging at you.

It sounds counterintuitive, but beware of your forward progress. Once you begin to speculate on the possibilities, the trek diverges and is riddled with what-if's and choices. Argh …. Complex again. Rein it in, Tonto.

When Annie searched inwardly for what she knew to be a fact, she articulated her desire to live overseas. In simple terms, we thought we might be able to make that the desired outcome. Again, simple by stating what we now knew: present dismal career and enticing desired outcome.

Our coaching sessions led to unearthing a little more at a time, such as crafting her unique value proposition to a potential employer. Although she was excited at the prospect of a big move, deciding on an actual destination was somewhat daunting. Back to simple: what would be the criteria for a city or country that might be a good destination for you to live and work? Baby steps.

If your tendency is to become overwhelmed in transition, the simplify strategy may be ideal for you. No extra charge. Wink.

Does the thought of simplifying the transition in front of you give you a sense of relief? If so, what is the high-level view that would streamline your situation? Describe it here.

_____

_____

_____

_____

_____

_____

_____

_____

Coping Strategy: Journal the Positive

When you want to ensure that someone will believe you, begin it with "Research indicates…"

Research indicates that affirming the good things that happen in your day create an elevated sense of satisfaction with your life and increased happiness. It's true.

Journaling can be a terrific coping mechanism to trigger positive enough feelings to overshadow the sense of dread you may be experiencing in your transition. And it's just a healthy habit for a more sustained happy life. Just ask Oprah.

You'll also realize other benefits of a more positive outlook by increasing your ability to problem solve, exhibiting more creativity, and realizing better health. The cold virus is fought off more effectively in happy people! Research indicates!

A positive outlook can be achieved by being more grateful of what you do have in your life that is good. Enter … the journal, whether it be a blank bound book, or post-its on your bathroom mirror.

Some tips for journaling:

- Recall something good that happened in your day or the past few days and begin writing without worrying about making it look perfect or too accurate.
- Being more specific in your writing will drive you more deeply into the goodness of the event.
- Include descriptive words, especially those that capture the 5 senses of the situation. What did it feel, smell, look, taste, or sound like?
- Write about people instead of things, although some materialistic items can bring happiness because they enhance a relationship or create experiences and memories.

No judging! If you've got a crazy busy schedule but you took 2 hours to binge-watch American Pickers yesterday, be grateful for it! Don't punish yourself.

Decide how you can regularly journal, but in a way that works for you and will not stress you out if you miss it. If you are the artistic type, check out Brené Brown's art journaling. It uses crayons, markers, tape, and all kinds of fun grade-school tools that make our lives colorful.

If you do not already, would you like to start journaling? If so, let's hear the task that will get you started, and when you'll get going on it.

_____

_____

_____

_____

_____

In fact, grab a few positive things that have happened to you in the past 24 hours and write them down here.

_____

_____

_____

_____

_____

_____

_____

_____

Coping Strategy: Wine

I asked my friends about their particular coping strategies, and Marit said hers was wine. Then she made me include it in the book.

She and most of my friends are Winas. And there's actually a decent little coping strategy in that. Wine is a pleasure. And it's often the means to a social bond. Do not underestimate your support system as a coping strategy, whether it includes alcoholic beverages or not. In the middle of it is girlfriend therapy, which facilitates progress.

I'm not a Psychologist, but I am sleeping with one, and he would promote this approach to managing transitions. Then again, *he* is a Wino, so that just makes us co-dependent. But that's okay. (Please note that I am not condoning alcohol if it provides a problem in your life. Really.)

At the heart of friend therapy is a pair of rewards, something that you get back as a bonus to their friendship. The interaction provides you with two critical elements: **empathy** for your position, and **ideas** to move forward.

Empathy and Ideas

Empathy is a natural healer. It reflects back to you a validation of your feelings. Your girlfriends check the stuck state you may be in by confirming it verbally and *whoa*-ing and *oh-yeah*-ing right along with you. It gives you a sense of approval.

A load of ideas for a successful transition for you often closely follow the empathy session. They are filled with "have you tried?" and "are you going to?" Sometimes you really luck out with a "I'll give you the cabin for a few days if you need to get away." Bonus!

Hey, I dare you to find a book written by a man that includes a coping mechanism that involves a tip of this nature, especially the girlfriend part.

When is your next girl time? If you don't have one scheduled, would you like to use this coping mechanism to see that your empathy and ideas needs get met? What'll you do to accomplish that?

_____

_____

_____

_____

_____

_____

_____

9 GAINING CONFIDENCE

While we women were sitting around waiting for the invention of diuretics, spandex, and self-help confidence-building products, we relied on our own assurance to prop up our ego.

In modern day, I'm afraid not much has changed, although Chardonnay is abundant and now we have Spanx® .

I don't think of ego as a term I'd tie to women, but I do think of self-doubt as peering its ugly little head into the scene. In the midst of change, it's not so much about ego as it is about assurance and the fortitude to push forward.

For many reasons, self-confidence in a woman can look dramatically different than in a man. Same for lack of self-confidence.

This chapter will take you through the major concepts to put you back on track to a confident you during an unpredictable transition in your life.

Know Yourself

We start with the compass to all your surroundings ... yourself.

Being "self aware" means understanding that you probably have a certain persona in your life. This includes how you are perceived in your marriage, your workplace, your social settings, your travels, etc. That persona usually doesn't vary much from setting to setting. The key to being self-aware is knowing what your persona is.

I know that my persona is sometimes intimidating because I am pretty confident. I have a large personality that can be threatening to women who are not confident. But, it took me years to figure that out. Females who feel I take too much control of a situation do not respond well to me. I have learned to assess the women in my environment before I actually do anything first and then I ensure that I communicate with warmth and care so that they know I have their interests at heart. I am not rolling over them. I don't change who I am, I just take others into consideration before making emotional or intellectual moves.

Take the time to really ask yourself what your persona is. Are you a pleaser? Are you aggressive? Are you a push-over? You get the idea. If you really don't know, then ask a good friend to give you a gentle description.

"Hey Deborah, how do you see me? Don't *completely* tell me like it is. Take the edge off, will ya?"

or

"Hey Deborah, remember that time when I shoved you aside at that shoe sale? Is that how you see the real me?"

or best yet

"Hey Deborah, I am really struggling on getting myself through this change and I could use some feedback. When I am in the midst of a transition, does it seem like I handle it well?"

Then dig a little deeper. Toss in a probing questions like

"If I were to manage myself better, what would be one recommendation you would give me?"

or

"Are there times when it looks like I am a little shaky in my confidence?"

Be open to feedback. It's important to listen here. This information will be valuable to you for the rest of your life.

In particular listen to that squeaky little voice in your head that suggests insecurity. How well do you know HER? Is there a self-doubt that lurks under the surface? Is there a behavior that you're struggling in identifying?

The other aspect of Know Yourself is the value that you bring to the table. Enter my friend Marvella -- fictitious name, as if that's not obvious.

Marvella had a fine job working in production for a company. After several years that company went out of business, through no fault of hers, of course. Subsequently, Marvella started a small business with a friend, both thinking that they could make a decent living as entrepreneurs.

The new business got off to a lukewarm start. Nevertheless, she told herself that business took time, effort, and endurance. She and her friend held out with an optimistic attitude.

After a brief two years, what seemed like an exciting idea, turned into a disaster. Marvella had sunk most of her life savings into this prospective endeavor, and it had seemed promising. She soon discovered that her business partner had lied to her and taken all her money. Her aspirations suddenly vanished.

With no job, she slinked away, back into a position at a company where she had previously worked, but in a new role. She was humiliated and saddened, but at least the new job could provide something she had missed … security.

In this new position, Marvella was bringing new assets to the table, having now developed skills beyond the earlier occupation. In fact, she was savvy enough to negotiate a commission on top of her base salary.

As her new job took her nationally, she gained some exposure to other organizations. Movers and shakers saw the value or her honed skills.

So guess who was the last one to recognize that value? Yep. She was.

Marvella still lived in the past, seeing herself as a mediocre player. Then throw in the failed business, and the fiasco was burned into her own view of capability, obscuring her confidence.

An outside person would easily see how her skills and abilities out-valued the job she currently held. She was now overqualified. In fact, her talent was so easily recognized by others that it was not unusual for her to receive job offers or be wooed with career opportunities.

Funny thing is, they were often companies where she could not picture herself for two reasons. First, she didn't see herself as capable as they saw her. Second, those that were trying to recruit her looked demographically different than her. They were end-of-career white men so she would assume their positions were best fits for their demographic ... them pale, male and stale.

Marvella's belief system had not evolved. She was stuck in the old view of believing she was a failure.

A woman's ability to know herself is largely dependent on the clarity of her introspection.

Friend Tales

Telling a tale on Katie, here. Katie was born with the ability to gather a group of people and engage them in social interaction that always results in that group being better. It's that simple. Katie's groups might be better at problem solving, debating, cooking, or just laughing, but it is a skill she is aware of and uses every day to help others.

As she becomes more self-aware, she better knows how to self-regulate, she can motivate others, and she is empathetic. Her social skills lead her to use and build upon the other skill sets. In plain words, she is a physically small person with a large personality. That dichotomy can be quite disconcerting for unsuspecting women (and men!). But, her learned and practiced observation skills, combined with her empathy have given her the life skills to be a speaker, coach, leader, writer, negotiator and friend.

The morals of this story are two-fold: don't discount your social skills; and Katie is a blast to have around.

-- Anne

Know Your Self-Talk

Rebecca relishes in taking care of her infant granddaughter two afternoons a week. She takes off work as the CEO of a mid-sized company to coo, cuddle, babble, and fuss over the baby with all the delight of a mama chimp picking tiny insects from her darling's mop. It gives her such gratification.

Rebecca lapses into baby talk at work.

The good news is that Rebecca will soon get more time with the kiddos because she has been planning on retirement for a while. Like an alcoholic slowly entering an addictive state, Rebecca has seen many stages of leaving one sort of life and transitioning into another yet-to-be-defined phase.

These are the stages she has encountered (not necessarily in this order)

The Stages of Self-Talk Through a Transition

Freshness
"Oooooh how exciting! I could be retired and take all the time I want to do anything I want."

Identity
"I'm eager for the change. But I don't know what my new life should look like. What if I have no identity? What if I become only known as the lady that comes into the grocery store and squeezes kiwi's? Or if I succumb to sub-par reality TV series and never leave the couch?"

Abandonment

"Am I failing anyone by leaving them behind? What if I just sneak out of my job when they are distracted doing something with each other and let them fend for themselves? Would they feel abandoned? Would they fail miserably without me?"

Co-dependence

"I can't do it. I simply can't make the move. I have too much at stake here. And I am really scared."

Reality Check

"I'm not quite salivating to see the change happen like I once was, but the potential of a stable and rewarding future is still attractive and within reach. If only I could get beyond the fears."

The Pivot

Somewhere in here a switch is made internally to go for the change. Reasoning is no longer about fear or loss, but instead about possibilities and reality.

Doomsday

"Really now, what's the worst that can happen? Would the world really turn on a different axis if I make this change? I mean really?"

Courage

"I am visualizing the future. I am going to focus only on that future without worrying about the past."

Damn the Torpedoes

"Screw it. I'm jumping."

The vast change in front of Rebecca includes a smooth succession of her leadership role, and the readying of the troops for her soon-to-be absence.

If you burned calories for every mind-changing effort you experienced, you'd be wearing a size 2. It's downright exhausting, and at some point quite taxing on you.

Think about what your self-talk is saying? Maybe no one listens to you, but you should definitely listen to yourself. I promise, you subconsciously are anyway.

Insights to my self-talk

_____

_____

_____

_____

_____

_____

_____

_____

Know What Motivates You

Motivation is a very personal thing. Much of it stems from what sort of person you are: an introvert or an extrovert. Extroverts are energized by being in the presence of others. It's as if their built-in solar panels were charged by those people orbiting around them. The more energy that's in a room, the better.

Introverts can be more complex, but may have an enhanced ability listen to their internal conversation and self-regulate more appropriately, at least it looks like that to the rest of us.

Finish this sentence:
I find the most satisfaction when I …..?

How you answer that sentence can be a tell-all. An effective way of tapping into your satisfaction trigger is to pay attention to how you respond to Facebook ads.

"New styles from Zappos"

"Find your high school boyfriend."

"Eliminate belly fat"
Tell me I'm not the only one that gets those?'

What must you be looking for? Is it filling a need? Or is it stretching a desired growth area?

EXERCISE

If you keep a gratitude journal, your answer to your motivations are right in front of you. Read your last few entries and look for a trend in the entries. Are you mostly gratified by interactions with others? Intermittent indulgences? Pleasant weather? Time to yourself? Time to stretch metaphorically or physically?

Your observations about what motivates you:

_____

_____

_____

_____

_____

_____

_____

_____

Take a look at your last credit card statement. What are the last 20 discretionary purchases? What do they tell you about what motivates you?

_____

_____

_____

_____

_____

_____

_____

_____

_____

_____

_____

An Interview on Motivation

Katie to Anne: Think of a time when you were most motivated to get something to change. What was it for and how did you use you your motivation to drive you?

Anne's response: Having received a degree in Human Resources, I started into the workforce as a recruiter for a large telemarketing company. There were four women in my office, one of which was a largely absent female boss.

The remaining three of us wanted her job, partly because we never saw her do anything.

She eventually left her position, which opened up my opportunity. Through very hard work, lots of late nights, and a lot of practice pretending the job was mine, I got it. I acted as if the promotion was in the bag, and that helped me behave as if I were performing the boss job. I think that when people saw the way I acted, they could visualize me doing that. It felt a bit like a performance, but I realized that was where my courage sprouted. Seeing myself act as a leader was as if I was in the wings seeing the role played out, and it reaffirmed my capabilities.

My new boss had promoted me, leaving the other two ladies in my wake. I had to take on the new job, manage the two not-so-happy women, and prove myself worthy.

My motivation was the job itself. It was what I had always wanted and dreamed it would be. The roadblocks were numerous and emotional. Persevering paid off. I had the job for ten years before I got married and had babies and had a whole new set of challenges and whiners were tossed at me. Next chapter!

Know the Situation

To best manage the current situation, we start with a revisit to a more ideal situation.

When you have achieved a win, or when you performed swimmingly in a tough fight, your confidence soars. We all know the feeling, wishing we could recreate it on demand. Your mind is clear, your sense of self is acute, and your personal mission feels nourished again.

When were you last on top of the world? Draw yourself a visual that takes you there, something that represents being high (not like that). Here's my visual: a plastic grocery bag gracefully aloft in a breeze. One woman's trash is another woman's treasure. That silly plastic Wal-Mart bag was the first thing that came to mind, so I'm going to stick with it. I see it now, floating through a blue sky.

That time when you were soaring feels great, doesn't it? Or at least it did at the time.

Confidence is the Memory of Success

My husband defines confidence as "The Memory of Success." The act of remembering when you did do it right can lead to better performance now.

For those times when you feel a little puny and need a bear hug, use your own history of fabulous accomplishments to boost the confidence. Find a stellar moment in your past that worked for you, where your performance flowed and your achievements were palpable. Many factors were probably in alignment for you, but don't compare what you had then in resources to what you may be dealing with now. The stars do not need to align in order for you to feel successful now. You alone can make the positive flow.

Neuroscience research has shown us that your mental posture in those situations can be more readily replicated when you relive the scene, using as many of your senses as possible, including emotion.

So when it is feeling like your plastic grocery bag has descended, completing its hop to finish off as wind whipped rubbish in a sticker bush, go back to the pinnacle of the flight. Therein lies the confident you.

EXERCISE

Think of a time when your confidence was very high. You were in the zone and could just tell that you were on the ball and fearless. Write everything about how you were feeling at the time, being sure to include as many of the five senses as possible.

_____

_____

_____

_____

_____

_____

_____

_____

_____

_____

_____

_____

_____

_____

_____

_____

_____

_____

_____

_____

_____

If this exercise works for you, you will have a sense of reliving the positive experience with confidence.

Manage Yourself

Managing yourself can be hard when designer shoes yell out at you from the store window. Physically managing yourself can be hard at times too, like running in the front door with a bulging bladder and button-fly jeans. Seriously, we tend to be rather impulsive sometimes, right girls? Know your abilities and know your limits.

Have you been heard saying that someone else had sent you into a state of uncontrolled fury? Or a co-worker's behavior had put you into a terrible mood?

My mom's favorite was "You kids are driving me batty!" If I heard that once, I heard it 1500 times.

These reactions indicate a lack of self-management (especially mom). After all, the other person isn't really driving you nuts, you are allowing the other person to get to you. You are in complete control of your reaction to others. In the least, you have a great influence over it.

Regulate not only your impulsive desires, but your time, your energy, your intellect, as well.

Now turn on the confidence

If you want people to believe you, speak and write concretely and unambiguously. Our minds process concrete statements more quickly, and we associate quick and easy with true. When something can be more easily pictured, it's easier to recall, so it seems more true. An active verb tense is perceived as more concrete and believable than a passive verb, because passive is more abstract.

Affirmations: A Way To Tap Your Confidence

Beyond just speaking positively, I never really knew what affirmations were. I suppose the more your mom read The Little Engine That Could to you, the more it became seeded in your mind.

Consider an affirmation to be a positive statement about something that you want more for yourself. For example, you may know that you are strong in a changing environment, but you need to hear yourself say it more.

"I've done this so well before. I can see myself accomplishing it."

Or you want to face something that you are dreading. Maybe just one word sends the affirmed message to you.

"Courage, Katie. Courage."

Stuart Smalley's "smart enough, good enough, and by God people like me!" may have mocked the process, but I am not above seeing Smalley as a role model. I am goofy, too.

For a more actionable process, here's one offered by Dr. David Krueger (thanks again) that includes some mechanics of affirmations. He refers to it as an art as well as a science. I share my list, partially adapted from his art and science:

- Speak to yourself in the present tense.
- Use positive language, rather than negative imaging. For example, change "don't eat so many carbohydrates" to "limit breads to one per day."
- Translate "I'm not going to curse at work" to "my language will be dignified from now on."
- Make it about you. Make it personal.
- Draw upon any memory of success that may boost your confidence and assist in a specific visual.
- Bring in all 5 senses. Visualize the ideal outcome and how it smells, tastes, looks, sounds, and feels. Of course this could mean that the ideal future involves the positive smell of warm bagels. Play with it.
- Describe the emotion involved.
- Make your affirmation brief and specific.
- Involve action words because they better describe execution.

EXERCISE

Name a situation where you most struggle with fear and self-doubt?

_____

_____

_____

_____

_____

What are the dynamics of that scenario that might be causing your reaction?

_____

_____

_____

_____

_____

_____

_____

_____

_____

_____

How many of those dynamics have to do with something changing or a transition you're going through? For those that do, name the loss.

_____

_____

_____

_____

_____

_____

_____

Use the affirmation technique to set a goal for a positive outcome. State at least one affirmation here.

_____

_____

_____

_____

_____

_____

_____

_____

10 CLOSING THOUGHTS

One last moment of encouragement

Something drew you to this book. But if you haven't figured it out yet, I would guess that you'll be tapped again with another change soon and have the opportunity to take a further look at your reactions, your perceived loss, and the opportunities to set it in another light. I am hoping that I, with help from Anne and Carol, had something encouraging to offer regarding managing change, or at least something in a way to which you could relate.

Because of my years and years, okay fine, decades, of training and coaching and consulting with people, especially and mostly women, I had heard enough struggle with the concept of transitioning through life's processes. The ups and the downs that are so predictable. Who would have ever thought change was predictable.

So perhaps my message in this final chapter is my reaching out to you in a way that connects to you. In turn, I hope it enables you connecting to yourself. Carol and I have always stated at the website and through our tiny trainings that we call Monday Morning Detox, that we love our tribe members to give us feedback. The message in this chapter would be no exception to that.

And ... something about what connecting to you means to me

Most of the writing that I've ever done has been blogs and magazine articles. You can see one of my favorites at the Skirt Strategies website "Drinking at Work. A Good Idea." (http://skirtstrategies.com/leadership-for-women/drinking-at-work-a-good-idea/) My first book, *Skirt Strategies: 249 Success Tips for Women in Leadership*, was an easy collection of standalone tips, 249 to be exact. I had no book-like writing experience before that.

Skirt Strategies was a perfect format for a multitasking (read scatterbrained) mind like mine. In the several months that it took to write this *Brave Transitions* book, I developed an interesting intimacy for my would-be readers. After stepping away occasionally from a writing bender, I found myself eager to get back to these chapters because I felt close to those of you that would be listening to me. It is an interesting and certainly unique relationship, one that I believe novelist must cherish and grow addicted to.

I hope I get to do it again with you.

The 5 "BE"s of Power and Influence

Here's your final confidence builder. I have named it The 5 "BE"s of Power and Influence. Go out and do it.

To build up self-confidence, consider where you see your influence in your world.

There are many misconceptions about power, sources of valid power, and how a woman's power is easily gained but not often exerted. If your power and influence in intact, it will endorse your composure in even the most challenging scenarios.

BE CONNECTED
- Begin with a laundry list of your most utilized network. Who is in it?
- Identify those that could be accessed more often. Take them to coffee. Send an email asking for their opinion on something.
- List others that could or should be in your network. Set a goal to approach them more or involve them.

BE KNOWLEDGABLE
- Describe the one thing that you are most known for.
- Are you letting others know that it's an area of expertise for you? (and don't play the "that's too conceited" move)
- How are you using your expertise to help others look good?

BE VISIBLE

- Use your name wherever you can, such as on reports or emails that may get circulated. Make it obvious.
- Get out there as a speaker. See the website for ideas.
- Attend events and people will think you get around … in a good way.

BE UNIQUE

- Think about one thing that people may come to you for to get something done or to add uniqueness?
- How do you let them know your uniqueness?
- What is one area of uniqueness that you're building?

BE LIKEABLE

- Compliment others readily and with ease
- Give recognition to others when they achieve something
- Be agreeable

ABOUT THE AUTHOR

Katie K. Snapp

Katie is on a crusade to encourage to like-minded women who want to enjoy life more by just managing themselves a teensy bit better. Her recent work with Carol Wight and online training site *Skirt Strategies* has exposed her craving to reach out to women through books, speaking engagements, and online. Her first book, *Skirt Strategies: 249 Success Tips for Women in Leadership*, is a collection of simple tips, techniques, and reminders to lead self and others in a feminine and natural way.

She was born and raised in Kansas City, Missouri and now lives in Albuquerque, New Mexico. She received her Bachelors Degree in Electrical Engineering at Mizzou (Go Tigers).

As if it's not painfully obvious, Katie is eager and available to speak to groups of women, or even humor mixed groups of men and women, to encourage and motivate.

ABOUT THE CONTRIBUTING AUTHORS

Anne Potter Russ

Having graduated from Mizzou, you'd think Anne would have a degree from their well-known journalism school. However, Anne Potter Russ, matriculated from the University of Missouri with a degree in Counseling and Human Relations instead. Putting that degree to good use, she worked in the HR field for ten years with The Signature Group, a since-defunct division of the long-gone Montgomery Ward company (not her fault). After getting married and created two wonderful children who are now in college, Anne worked in non-profit fundraising and event coordination, as well as editing a Kansas City magazine. She now contributes to local magazines, blogs and books as a freelance writer. She is also dying to drive an RV around the country with her husband, and he is currently resisting. The dogs are onboard, though.

Carol M. Wight

At 21, Carol opened her first restaurant. By the time she was 30 she owned three successful restaurants with 150 employees. Utilizing entrepreneurial skills and restaurant expertise, she became an international consultant in destinations like Abu Dhabi, and Tokyo. Carol eventually became the CEO of the New Mexico Restaurant Association, running a 1,100 member trade organization where she advocated to improve the conditions of the industry in New Mexico. Through her work as an entrepreneur and advocate she realized that women entrepreneurs like herself needed a membership organization to support their road to success. She joined forces with author Katie Snapp to bring her first book *Skirt Strategies: 249 Success Tips for Women in Business* to life in a supportive membership community, empowering women to reach their full potential so they can obtain the leadership positions they deserve.

Made in the USA
Charleston, SC
19 October 2014